The Unseen World of the
HOLY SPIRIT

DATE DUE

**This item is Due on
or before Date shown.**

2017

The Unseen World of the
HOLY SPIRIT

Experiencing the
Fullness of God's Presence

Frank Bailey

DESTINY IMAGE® PUBLISHERS, INC.

P.O. Box 310, Shippensburg, PA 17257-0310

"Speaking to the Purposes of God for this Generation and for the Generations to Come."

This book and all other Destiny Image, Revival Press, Mercy Place, Fresh Bread, Destiny Image Fiction, and Treasure House books are available at Christian bookstores and distributors worldwide.

For a U.S. bookstore nearest you, call 1-800-722-6774.

For more information on foreign distributors, call 717-532-3040.

Or reach us on the Internet: **www.destinyimage.com**

ISBN 10: 0-7684-2486-0

ISBN 13: 978-0-7684-2486-7

For Worldwide Distribution, Printed in the U.S.A.

2 3 4 5 6 7 8 9 10 11 / 09 08 07

Endorsements

I will never forget the fax that told me to "Call Frank and ask what is so funny." I had known him for over ten years and had never heard him laugh. I called expecting a joke and found a man who had been touched by the Holy Spirit. You can not separate revival and joy. The psalmist teaches us that we are revived so that we may rejoice in God (see Ps. 85:6). I will always be thankful to God for sending Frank Bailey to me and to our church, bringing revival and the joy that flows with it. We will never be the same.

Dr. David E. Sumrall, Pastor
Cathedral of Praise
Manila, Philippines

The proof of revival is change. What many people fail to realize is that God does not want us to experience a temporary change; rather He wants to mold us into His image permanently. Having known Frank Bailey since 1994, and also having the privilege of ministering to his people at Victory Fellowship, I can testify that Pastor Frank and the church have not only been changed by the power of God, but also have continued in the revival and are having a tremendous impact on their community.

Steve Solomon, Pastor
Riverwalk Fellowship
Host of "Praise in the Night" radio program
Fort Worth, Texas

It's been a personal joy to watch the growth and progress of Frank and Parris Bailey. I first met them in the mid-seventies as a part of the Jesus People movement. They stood out in a crowd and caught my attention with their joy, their enthusiasm, and their quest for God's supernatural power. I met them again in the mid-eighties while they were pastoring a fast-growing church in Metairie, Louisiana. Again, I was impressed with their aggressive leadership. They had expanded their facilities four times in ten years. They always found their driving force in an aggressive evangelism, a vibrantly-alive worship, and a commitment to honor the inspired word of Scripture. It was only natural that the current refreshing renewal should sweep over their congregation.

At present, the church is experiencing rapid growth, healthy evangelism, dynamic worship and an atmosphere that is charged with the presence of the Lord. It's awesome to be part of a divine visitation. The members and friends of Victory Fellowship are in the middle of an exciting move of God's Holy Spirit. Pastor Bailey's new book, *The Unseen World of the Holy Spirit,* is an account of where they came from, where they are, and their God-given vision for where they are going. It's almost like a diary or a book of chronicles telling what the Lord has done and is doing.

Dick Mills, Evangelist

Frank Bailey writes simply, profoundly, precisely, and although until now his works have been brief, they are replete with wisdom and easily understood. So well is this done, that the reader feels satisfied that he sees what the author intends us all to see. One has the feeling, as one eagerly moves from page to page, that the travel agent (author) on this journey has not only been where he is seeking to guide us, but that he understands why he has been there.

I expect from the pen of Frank Bailey a long and rich series of helpful works that will help us all survive and thrive in whatever conditions we find ourselves. This will be the great pulpit from which the world hears the true gospel of the Kingdom, and it is open to us all!

Jack Taylor, President
Dimension Ministries
Melbourne, Florida

Dedication

To the members of Victory Fellowship. Your love for the presence of God is encouraging and contagious.

Contents

SECTION TWO
Proclaiming the Glory of God

Foreword

When Pastor Frank Bailey asked me to write the foreword for his book, *The Unseen World of the Holy Spirit*, which looks back over the previous several years of revival in his life and ministry, he sent the manuscript to me to read. As I read it, I found myself rejoicing over all the wonderful things that God has done!

I met Pastor Frank Bailey during one of our meetings in Rockwall, Texas, in 1994. I remember well the first week of meetings that we held the following year in New Orleans. Approximately 30,000 people walked through the doors of Victory Fellowship in six days, and some of them did not even make it through the doors—there was no more space in the building for them—they sat outside listening to the services over the sound system. The move of God in Victory Fellowship has not only touched New Orleans, but also Louisiana, other parts of the U.S., and various locations overseas. I rejoice at how God has used Pastor Frank Bailey to ignite a fire in the Philippines, which continues to this day, as well as in many other countries of the world.

I have come to love and respect Frank Bailey, and I am happy to be counted as his friend. He is a sincere and anointed man of God. I trust that this book will bless you as it did me.

Rodney M. Howard-Browne
President and Founder
Revival Ministries International Inc.
Tampa, Florida

Section One

Experiencing the Glory of God

Introduction

People have discussed and prayed for "the Coming Revival" for as long as I can remember. "When will it come?" "What will it be like?" "What will be the emphasis?" Everyone talks about revival, but so many have different ideas about what it will be like. Some say it will be centered on repentance; others say miracles of healing. But most agree that a harvest of unusual proportions will characterize "the Coming Revival." All sorts of opinions have been offered, but no one really knows for sure.

When revival begins, will you embrace it, run for cover, or stand by as a spectator? Jesus started a big controversy when He got up in the synagogue and proclaimed, *"Today this scripture is fulfilled..."* (Luke 4:21) because today meant now, not tomorrow or someday. Today meant that they had to decide, with a yes or no, whether or not they would believe. You must decide for yourself. Why? Because revival is chaotic. Revival means a rushing, mighty wind, tongues of fire, intoxicated behavior, and speaking in other languages. Laughing, crying, shaking, falling, and running have accompanied revival for centuries. These manifestations, which generally cause controversy, were seen in the upper room, in the ministries of John Wesley, George Whitfield, Jonathan Edwards, Evan Roberts, and in the Azusa Street revival under W.J. Seymour.

We can no longer just talk about "the Coming Revival" because the wind of God has begun to blow across the earth again. Revival fires are breaking out across America, Canada, and literally the whole world. Reports of revival are being heard across Europe, Central and South America, Australia, Africa, and Asia. All of the earth is experiencing the beginning of the latter rain of the Holy Spirit. The question you must ask yourself is, "Will I embrace revival?" Will you ignore the critics and launch out into the deep? The wind has begun to blow. The horizon is dark with clouds of a great storm. The lightning is flashing in the sky. The first drops of rain have begun to fall. Revival is upon us. As you read this book, let the rain of God begin to fall on you. Refreshment and change will result as you embrace the revival.

CHAPTER I

Could This Be Revival?

He changes a wilderness into a pool of water, and a dry land into springs of water (Psalm 107:35 NASB).

I thought I knew the power of God. My wife and I were born again in August 1973. At our conversion experience, God delivered us from drugs, alcohol, nicotine, and many other sins. For the next four years, I attended a Full Gospel Bible school, and I was involved with street evangelism both during school and after my graduation. In 1979, my wife, Parris, and I pioneered a church, Victory Fellowship, in a suburb of New Orleans. Over the years, thousands of lives were touched and changed through our ministry. Of course I knew about the power and anointing of the Holy Spirit, or at least I thought I knew.

We had gone through building projects, writing books, holding church growth conferences, and doing everything a "successful" ministry should do. Our people loved us; our children were wonderful, and we lived in a nice house. We had a wonderful church, and we had done just about everything we could to boost church growth. We traveled the world and loved all we did in ministry, but we failed to realize that we had sprung a leak.

Somewhere, somehow, during our 20-some years of ministry, we came up dry, dead, and empty. The years of pastoring had begun to take a heavy toll on my life. The ministry had gradually become a job, and the joy of ministry had slipped away. I was tired of dealing with people's problems, and for the first time, in August 1994, I considered pursuing other interests. There was no way I could continue leading my church when I was running out of gas.

During this time of soul searching, I met Pastor Rick Shelton at a minister's conference. I had heard of Rick's ministry in St. Louis, and had great respect for him and for what the Lord had done through him over the years. He began to share with me what had recently happened in his life. He told me he had been touched by the Lord and he had been changed. Those words, "I have been changed," began to repeat over and over in my mind. Pastors don't talk like that. Pastors talk about programs and plans for church growth. Pastors don't talk about being changed or about their need for change. Surely something had touched him, and I had to find out what it was.

Some of the other ministers at the meeting began to talk about revival. They discussed meetings that they had attended conducted by Rodney Howard-Browne, a missionary-evangelist from South Africa. Each one told a story similar to Rick Shelton's. Their lives had been transformed. Revival seemed to be in the air. If this was re-vival, I had to know for sure. I hoped this move of God would be the answer to the struggle raging in my heart.

Rodney Howard-Browne was conducting revival meetings in Rockwall, Texas, at Church on the Rock, during the month when everything in my life seemed to be coming to a head. I knew I had to go and see for myself.

My ministry had always been characterized, I thought, by stability. I knew what I believed and tried to stay away from the fads that come through the Body of Christ. I was skeptical of the rumors I had heard—laughing, running, shaking, and the like. Because of my skepticism, I told the Lord, "Lord, I want to see three things in these meetings. I want to see repentance, salvation, and humility in this evangelist." With these conditions made very clear, I went to Rockwall to check out this "revival."

After my arrival at Church on the Rock, I found a safe seat near the back of the congregation. The service was already in progress and chaos was breaking out everywhere. People were laughing, crying, shaking, and making all sorts of noises. All but one thing made this atmosphere uncomfortable for me; the presence of the Lord was very strong and confirmed to me that these meetings were the work of the Holy Spirit. The more I sat in the meeting that night, the stronger the Lord's presence became. As the night went on, I began to fall under conviction. The Lord began to put His finger on areas in my life that needed change. I began to repent, and suddenly realized the first condition that I placed before the Lord had been met. Repentance was obviously part of this revival.

As the service drew to an end that night, a salvation altar call was given. I remember thinking, "No one will respond tonight. There is too much chaos. The unbelievers, if they're still here, will never respond." Was I ever in for a surprise that night! Over 100 people came forward for salvation and rededication (this was only one night of a daily six-week revival). I watched the people go forward, and looked at their faces. These were not church people but people from the world who were obviously being touched by the Lord. As I watched the scene unfold, I heard the Lord gently remind me, "Your second condition has been met."

After the service that night, one of the ushers took me to see the pastor, my friend, Mike Hankins. I was shocked when I saw Mike and his wife, Vickie. Neither one could communicate very well; both were obviously very drunk in the Holy Ghost. Mike introduced me to Rodney Howard-Browne. He was not what I expected. For years I had been around famous preachers, and far too many had a very arrogant, untouchable side to them. But Rodney was the biggest kid I had ever seen. He was singing Holy Ghost drinking songs and was obviously excited about the things of God. The Holy Spirit gently reminded me, "That is the third condition you placed on Me."

For the next two days I sat in the revival meetings, soaking in the presence of the Lord. I returned home but went back to Rockwall again, this time with about 20 people from my staff. Everyone was excited and expectancy was in the air. No one knew that all of our lives were about to be changed forever.

In one of the morning services, Rodney called for ministers from Louisiana to come forward for prayer. I was ready. I went forward and began to lift my hands and worship the Lord. I had never fallen under the power before (pretty strange for someone who had pastored a Pentecostal church for 17 years), and I was not about to fall down now. Suddenly, I felt someone's hands laid upon me, and I found myself flat on my back on the floor. Slightly embarrassed, I tried to get up, only to find that I was stuck to the floor. The next thing I knew, waves of glory came upon me, and I began to laugh. I laughed and laughed and the more I laughed, the more intoxicated I became. This was all new to me. Here I was, stuck to the floor, drunk and laughing, and I didn't even care. In those moments, God changed my life in many ways beyond my greatest expectations.

Over the next day, God touched my entire staff with this revival anointing. Each one had experiences similar to mine; none of them would ever be the same. When the time came to return to our church in New Orleans, we had no idea what was about to happen.

That next Sunday, the wind of God began to blow into our building. I tried to tell the congregation what had happened but had a very difficult time. The more I talked, the more intoxicated I became. During the service, I had to be picked up off of the floor several times. The power of God began to touch people throughout the church. As I laid hands on people, a mighty anointing began to fall upon each one. Hundreds of people were laid out all over the floor. Some were out under the power the entire day. They were laughing, trembling, and crying, but most of all, they were changing. That Sunday was the beginning of a new day in our church. At the time of this publication, fourteen years have passed and our church is still experiencing the manifest presence of the Lord. This is truly revival!

CHAPTER 2

Why All the Laughter?

Therefore with joy shall ye draw water out of the wells of salvation (Isaiah 12:3).

W hy all the laughter? What does laughter have to do with revival anyway? These questions, and many others, ran through my head when I began to hear about the spreading move of God. I had always cautiously avoided the pitfalls, the side journeys, and majoring on minor issues that have frequently plagued the Full Gospel movement from as far back as I can remember. When I heard about the laughing, all I could think was, "Oh no, here we go again." Those "laughing meetings" seemed to be just another crazy charismatic side journey, as far as I was concerned. They spoke of everything I tried to stay away from. How wrong I was.

When God touched me in the Rockwall revival meetings, joy poured out of my innermost being. As I was lying on the floor, waves of glory came upon me and rivers of joy began to flow out of me. I laughed and laughed as I was filled to overflowing with the Holy Ghost. For the next month I became a "drunken" preacher. I would become so filled with joy as I began to preach that many times I would find myself on the floor, overcome by the power of God. The Holy Ghost was overhauling my life.

On the first Sunday after returning from the ministers' meeting, I received a phone call from my brother. He knew all the pressure I had experienced pastoring the church. On that Sunday as I gave the salvation altar call and people began to come forward, I was overcome with joy. Seeing people give their lives to Christ put me over the top, and I fell under the power of God. I was able to gather myself together and lead these precious people to Christ in prayer, but I continued to laugh and rejoice as I laid hands on anyone who wanted ministry. When my brother called, he called out of concern. He thought I was losing my mind. Actually, I was coming out of my mind and into my spirit. Though he was initially concerned, my brother has remained in our church. Surprisingly few people left our church when the eruption began, but many new people began to come as a result of the outpouring of the Holy Spirit.

Why all the laughter? The Scriptures provide many examples of joy and laughter. In Psalm 2:4, God sits in the heavens and laughs at His enemies. If God can laugh at His enemies, we can surely laugh with Him. Another example of laughter is found in the story of the birth of Abraham's son, Isaac. In Genesis chapter 17, Abraham is discouraged. He is 99 years old and his wife, Sarah, still had no child. The Lord had promised them a child more than 20 years before. Not only had God promised them a child, but He had also promised that nations would come from their descendants. It appears to Abraham that God's promises would never be fulfilled. But God visits Abraham, and Abraham falls on his face laughing (see Gen. 17:17).

In Genesis 18, God visits Abraham and Sarah again and reiterates His promise. When Sarah hears that she will become pregnant, she can not believe her ears. She thought, "I could not become pregnant when I was a young woman. I am past the age of bearing children. Now I am 90 years old, how can I become pregnant?" As she ponders the possibility of becoming pregnant, she begins to laugh.

Within one year, Isaac was born. In Genesis 21, Sarah says that they would name their son Isaac (Hebrew for laughter), because everyone who heard the story of her late-in-life pregnancy would laugh with her.

Abraham and Sarah had gone through many disappointing years before their son was born. They had served the Lord for years, and yet it appeared that His promises would not be fulfilled. They had become depressed and disillusioned. Disappointment had stolen their joy. Just before Isaac's birth, God restored their joy with His presence.

In a similar way, God is visiting His people today. Many thousands of Christians have been depressed and disappointed with many things in their lives. Today God is visiting His people with His presence and restoring their joy. This joy makes Christianity fun again. The joy is back in our prayer, our Bible reading, and our church gatherings. Surely *"the joy of the Lord is our strength"* (see Neh. 8:10).

Isaac's life is a picture of the move of God. In Genesis 26:18, the Philistines had clogged up the wells that Abraham had dug. The wells represent our spirit and spiritual life. The Philistines represent the enemy and this present evil world. Just as the Philistines clogged up the wells, the world has clogged up God's flow in the Church, blocking the joy of God's people. But Isaac unclogged the wells. This present move of God is the ministry of Isaac. Remember, Isaac means laughter. This supernatural joy and laughter are sent by God to unclog our wells. With joy we are drawing forth water from the wells of salvation (see Isa. 12:3).

The Bible is filled with examples of joy and laughter. David rejoiced and danced before the ark (see 1 Chron. 15:25-29). He rejoiced when the offerings were received for the temple (see 1 Chron. 29:9). Jesus rejoiced greatly when the disciples gave their ministry report (see Luke 11:17-22). Paul rejoiced in prison (see Acts 16:25). Peter rejoiced during persecution. He spoke of joy unspeakable and the fullness of glory (see 1 Pet. 1:8). All of Heaven rejoices when one sinner repents (see Luke 15:10). Heaven is a place of laughter, joy, celebration, and rejoicing (see Psalm 2:4). Through this current outpouring of joy, God is putting a little bit of Heaven back in His Church.

One evening, the joy of the Lord spread through our service. People spontaneously broke out in Holy Ghost laughter all over the building. While listening to this wonderful sound, I heard the Lord say, "This is the sound of Heaven." As I reflected on that statement, I began to imagine Heaven. I pictured people singing and laughing by the thousands. Then I began to imagine the voice of God, the voice of many waters, breaking out in thunderous laughter (see Rev. 14:2). Heaven is filled with laughter! If God is laughing, why should we remain silent? Go ahead, have a laugh. Join in with God, His holy angels, all of the redeemed in Heaven, and all of His creation. Surely the heavens and the earth are rejoicing in the presence of the Holy One.

It's important how we enter a Holy Ghost service. If our cups are full of the world, the Holy Spirit won't be able to pour into us. We need to empty ourselves and hunger for the Lord. It is the same with our wells. We must unclog our wells, and only the Holy Ghost performs a really good Rotor-Rooter job. Are you willing to open yourself up to the Holy Spirit to see just how fragile you really are in comparison to God's unsearchable riches? When the Holy Spirit truly touches you, you can cry out as Paul did, "*Who shall separate us from the love of Christ? Shall tribu-lation, or distress, or persecution, or famine, or nakedness, or peril, or sword?*" (Rom. 8:35).

It is OK to laugh. Just open up your heart to the presence of the Lord. As He fills you, His joy will rise inside of you. Yield to His presence, and you will find yourself filled with His glory. Before you know it, you will experience God's unspeakable joy.

CHAPTER 3

Learning How to Drink

On the last day, that great day of the feast, Jesus stood and cried out saying, "If anyone thirsts, let him come to Me and drink. He who believes in Me, as the Scripture has said, out of his heart will flow rivers of living water" (John 7:37-38 NKJV).

In this passage, Jesus tells us to drink the living water that flows from the throne of God. He was not speaking of a one-time experience, but of a lifestyle. You can actually learn how to drink in the glory of God. The more time you spend drinking in this glorious river, the more you will be changed.

Shortly after God renovated my life through this revival, I attended some revival meetings conducted by Rodney Howard-Browne in St. Louis. These meetings were at Christian Life Center, where Rick Shelton pastors. After several days of drinking in the glory of God, I had an interesting experience. I went to lunch with Pastor Rick and Brother Rodney after one of the morning meetings (that morning meeting actually went until 3 P.M.). At the end of our lunch, we were saying our good-byes outside the restaurant, which happened to be in a mall. The next thing I knew, I fell on the floor laughing and rolling around. What an interesting situation, a pastor rolling around drunk in front of Lord and Taylor Department Store. I was so amused by watching the expressions on people's faces as they passed by. It is amazing how little you care about what people think when you are in His presence.

As I returned home from St. Louis, I realized some lessons that the Holy Spirit was teaching me. He was showing me that I could learn how to drink of His presence anytime and anywhere. He was also showing me that the more I drank, the drunker I would become, and that the drunker I became, the more I would change. I want to share with you some things I have learned about drinking.

First, worship plays a key role in drinking of His presence. Second Chronicles chapter 5 illustrates the powerful influence of worship:

And it came to pass when the priests came out of the Most Holy Place (for all the priests who were present had sanctified themselves, without keeping to their divisions), and the Levites who were the singers, all those of Asaph and Heman and Jeduthun, with their sons and their brethren, stood at the east end of the altar, clothed in white linen, having cymbals, stringed instruments and harps, and with them one hundred and twenty priests sounding with trumpets—indeed it came to pass, when the trumpeters and singers were as one, to make one sound to be heard in praising and thanking the Lord, and when they lifted up their voice with the trumpets and cymbals and instruments of music, and praised the Lord, saying: "For He is good, for His mercy endures forever," then the house of the Lord, was filled with a cloud, so that the priests could not continue ministering because of the cloud; for the glory of the Lord filled the house of God (2 Chronicles 5:11-14 NKJV).

The priests began to worship the Lord and blow their trumpets. As they did, the tangible presence of God came into the temple. The priests could not stand up because of the overwhelming presence of God. In the same way today, worship ushers in God's presence. When we worship Him, His glory falls upon us. This new outpouring has renovated the music ministry at our church. Our musicians, choir, and worship leaders have received a double dose of the anointing of the Holy Spirit. Many times during worship, the choir, musicians, or people in the congregation will end up on the floor, overwhelmed by the glory of God. Worshiping is a wonderful way to drink from the river of life.

Another drinking tool that God has given us is our prayer language. Praying in tongues has many benefits and purposes. One of these benefits is a heightened awareness of the presence of the Holy Spirit. Many times when people pray in tongues, they are in a pouring out mode. Many Christians have used their prayer language in intercession only. One of the great purposes of our prayer language is to build us up. As Paul wrote, "*He who speaks in a tongue edifies himself...*" (1 Cor. 14:4 NKJV).

Jesus taught about receiving the Holy Spirit in John chapter 20. He breathed on the disciples and said, "*Receive the Holy Spirit...*" (see John 20:22). Receiving the Holy Spirit is very similar to breathing. We need to inhale as well as exhale. Learn to inhale, or receive, in your prayer time, and you will find yourself basking in the sunlight of His glory.

Many pastors and Christian leaders have a very hard time receiving. I was no exception. It seemed as if I had totally forgotten how to receive. My whole life had been caught up in giving. I was preaching, counseling, and even in prayer I was always pouring out.

In this revival, I have learned how to receive again. What a blessing to be able to soak in the presence of the Lord. Now I can pray in tongues in the receiving mode and step over into the realms of God.

Another way I have learned to drink is through the wonderful joy of the Lord. Peter talked about *"joy unspeakable and full of glory"* (1 Pet. 1:8). This joy is not human joy but the joy of the Lord. Isaiah wrote about the joy of the anointing. *"Therefore with joy you will draw water from the wells of salvation"* (Isa. 12:3 NKJV).

The water in this passage refers to the anointing. The wells refer to our spirit, or our innermost being. This verse teaches that there is a supernatural joy that literally draws the anointing out of our innermost being. We may not understand, but God has chosen to use joy as a tool to draw out the anointing. In many of our services, the joy of the Lord will begin to break out among the people. As I look around, I see some people doing their best not to laugh. The Holy Spirit will be all over them and they will do everything they can not to laugh. If you think about it, they are actually resisting the flow of the Holy Ghost.

Yield to His touch. When the joy comes, begin to laugh. Some people say that they have a silent joy. That does not make sense. When people are filled with joy, they laugh. Laughter is the voice of joy. It is OK to laugh. It is OK to rejoice and dance and shout. Go ahead and yield to the joy. Go ahead and laugh. As you laugh, you will become aware of His presence. Out of your innermost being will begin to flow rivers of living water (see John 7:28).

So, you see you can drink anytime you want. You can worship into His presence. You can pray in tongues and step over. You can even laugh and fall into the river. Let us make a quality decision. Let us decide to drink ourselves into the glory realm. I don't want to sip; I want to drink deeply from His awesome river. As we do, we will be forever changed into His glorious likeness.

It is when we get satisfied that we get into trouble. We must stay hungry: hungry for more of Him, hungry to change, hungry to learn about the bottomless things of God, and hungry to press through the crowds and grab hold and never let go. As the psalmist wrote, "*God— you're my God! I can't get enough of you!* (Ps. 63:1 TM).

CHAPTER 4

Love the Lord

"Hear, O Israel: the Lord our God, the Lord is one! You shall love the Lord your God with all your heart, with all your soul, and with all your strength"

(Deuteronomy 6:4-5 NKJV).

This passage of Scripture describes the greatest commandment and responsibility contained in the Scriptures. It also contains the greatest blessing for Christians. When we begin to actively and passionately love the Lord, we are launched into another realm of freedom and liberty. Most Christians are bound with rules, programs, and rituals. These rituals come in Protestant and Catholic forms. They come in Evangelical and Pentecostal forms. Only when we learn to love the Lord with our spirit, soul, and our strength can we step out of religious bondage into the glorious liberty of Christ.

First, we must love the Lord with our heart and our spirit. Man is created in the image of God. We are not animals but spirit beings. Because we are spirits, we can fellowship with God who is also spirit. This is what Jesus meant when He said, "*God is a spirit and they that worship him must worship in spirit and in truth*" (John 4:24). This present revival is causing people to become aware of the spiritual realm. We are becoming aware of the angels, who are spirit beings, but most of all we are becoming aware of the awesome Holy Spirit. He is pouring Himself out on the earth, and we are learning how to tap into His presence.

Recently, the Lord explained this to me through an illustration. He reminded me of a radio, that can potentially receive many signals. But in order to benefit from the many possible selections, you must turn the dial of the radio to pick up the different frequencies. If your radio dial was stuck, you would have to settle for listening to that one station, permanently. The Lord told me that for years I had not tuned in my spirit to the proper frequency. He had been broadcasting His anointing, but I was tuned in to the wrong frequency. Once you have been born again by the Holy Spirit, your spirit comes alive. It is then when we have to learn to receive more and more of the Holy Ghost by tuning in to the proper channel.

So what does it mean to love the Lord with all of my heart? It means pursuing His presence and worshiping Him with other tongues and with my understanding. It means opening my heart up to this new intimacy. It means pursuing fellowship with the Father of Spirits, the wonderful Holy Spirit.

God also said that we must love Him with all of our soul. Our soul is our intellect, our will, and our emotions. The Body of Christ has had great teaching on renewing our minds and yielding our wills to the Lord. We have stressed those areas of the soul for many years. But the realms of the emotions have gone almost totally unexplored. In this current outpouring, however, people are discovering that we are emotional beings, that the

Lord created us to laugh and to cry. It is OK to love the Lord with all of our soul, including our emotions.

When our church first began to experience this outpouring, I noticed an interesting response in some individuals. Some were deeply overwhelmed with joy and found themselves swimming in the river of God. Others seemed to be "locked up" and would begin to cry when the anointing of the Lord would come upon them. This troubled some of the "criers." They wanted to enter in but could not seem to break through. As several weeks passed, the Lord began to show something to me. It was as if years of emotional hurts were inside of these people, and more and more of the hurts were coming out as they entered His presence.

After several weeks of meetings, many of their tears had turned into laughter. The Lord was putting on *"a garment of praise for the spirit of heaviness."* He was turning our *"mourning into dancing"* (Isa. 61:3; Ps. 30:11). It is OK to laugh or to cry. It is OK for us to display our emotions in church. Much of what we have called decent and orderly has been bondage and control. We are learning to be free in the presence of the Lord. Go ahead and love the Lord with all of your soul. Love Him in your tears. Love Him in your laughing and rejoicing.

The Lord also instructs us to love Him with all of our strength. He wants us to get involved physically. You can love Him by raising your hands, clapping, shouting, dancing, or running in His presence. I am learning to be more physical in my love for the Lord. During many songs, I will lie on the floor as I begin to worship the Lord. Initially I feel nothing, but before long I am lost in the realm of God's presence. Recently in one of our services, many of us began to prostrate ourselves before the Lord. As we loved on Him and expressed our humility before Him, His glory came down like a heavy blanket in the building. When the anointing began to lift, we realized that one and a half hours had passed. I remember being shocked, thinking I had been on the floor for only about 30 minutes. Time does not exist in His wonderful presence.

Actually, we cannot separate spirit, soul, and body. As we begin to love the Lord from one specific area of our being, our whole being is drawn into worship. Let me share one example with you. I was attending a revival meeting and found myself falling into a trance. (See Acts 10 for a biblical example of a trance.) The Lord was speaking to me about resting in Him and not striving. When I began to come around, I found that I had been frozen in a certain position for 30 minutes or more. As I was sharing my experience the following Sunday with our church, I began to imitate the position that I had been frozen in. Suddenly, I found myself experiencing the same anointing falling on me again. I began to understand that my whole being—spirit, soul, and body—were closely connected to each other. We can initiate worship from all parts of our beings.

There may be some things in your personal life that need to change. Maybe you used to bark at the kids, kick the dog, scream at traffic, and then become a television zombie—and that was on a good day! We all need to let the Holy Spirit invade our personal lives. It doesn't matter how you shake, rattle, and roll at church, if you don't let it bubble over and change your personal side. When I got saved in 1973, I went in with an attitude that I "surrendered all," knowing that I needed a complete overhaul.

Will you let the Holy Ghost become a mighty jackhammer, going where no man would dare? Let the fire of God change you! Cross over, out of the natural, and move into the supernatural. God will pour His oil upon you so that when the flesh rises up, it will just roll off of you. Often my wife and I have heard each other laughing uncontrollably in our sleep. God is changing us daily as we continue to surrender to Him.

Go ahead and love the Lord; shout for joy; clap your hands, and prostrate yourself in His presence. Run around the building or dance for Him. I promise you, God will not be offended.

Non-Christians will rarely be offended. Some religious people will probably be offended, but that is OK. They were also offended at Jesus. Go ahead and love the Lord with all of your heart, all of your soul, and all of your strength. When I was touched by this revival, I became more aware of the presence of God. Every time I worship or think about Him, I am overwhelmed with His glory. Suddenly, His presence is there. As a result of this, I have fallen in love with Jesus. He has called me back to my first love.

CHAPTER 5

Behind the Veil

Having therefore, brethren, boldness to enter into the holiest by the blood of Jesus, by a new and living way, which he hath consecrated for us, through the veil, that is to say, his flesh; and having an high priest over the house of God; let us draw near with a true heart in full assurance of faith, having our hearts sprinkled from an evil conscience and our bodies washed with pure water. Let us hold fast the profession of our faith without wavering; (for he is faithful that promised) (Hebrews 10:19-23).

One of the most awesome characteristics of the revival is the obvious presence of God. Many people touched by this revival have learned how to walk in the awareness of His presence. In Hebrews 10, the author talks about entering behind the veil. He says that the veil in the Old Testament temple symbolizes the flesh of man. Even though Jesus has opened the way into the presence of God for us, most Christians never learn how to enter behind the veil, and only a small number have learned to live behind the veil of His presence. What separates Christians from the presence of the Lord? What does this veil of flesh represent?

First, this veil speaks to us about the cares and desires of this present world. There are so many distractions to keep us from His presence, that is, in the world of the flesh. We have worries, fears, entertainment, personal goals, and ambitions, to mention just a few. These distractions separate us from the tangible presence of the Lord. These desires have to be replaced with a hunger for the Lord. When we begin to hunger and thirst for Him, we can push behind the veil.

This veil of flesh also speaks of religious traditions. Many of us are caught up in traditions, programs, and formats that make it highly unlikely for there to be a move of God. The traditions of man, regardless of how spiritual they appear to be, keep us from experiencing the real God. These traditions keep us from what Jesus called worshiping Him in spirit and in truth, or in reality. Many ministers have a set form and purpose in their services. These forms become a hindrance for the move of the Holy Ghost. For many years, I experienced this frustration in my ministry. I believed that I was on the cutting edge of worship and that I had a progressive full-gospel ministry. Little did I know that our progressive services were very predictable and rigid. Only after I was changed did I allow a spontaneous expression of worship and ministry to flow in our church. The veil of religion had blocked the move of the Holy Ghost. But now we are moving in the freedom and reality of the Holy Spirit. We are pressing in behind the veil.

The veil also speaks to us about time. In our fast-paced society, we have become extremely time conscious. The services in most churches can be predicted to end at a certain time. If the meeting goes much past that time, the people become restless and begin to look at their watches. How can God move in such a carnal environment? In order to move behind the veil, we must move beyond our user-friendly short services. We must take the time to wait upon the Lord. We must learn to sit quietly in His presence. As Isaiah wrote, "*But those who wait upon the Lord shall renew their strength, they shall mount up with wings like eagles, they shall run and not be weary, they shall walk and not faint*" (Isa. 40:31 NKJV). Many times people do not want to leave our services. Many linger for hours, enjoying the presence of the Lord. When you get one taste of life behind the veil, of life in His presence, time will begin to lose its importance.

In Romans chapter 8, Paul talks about walking in the Spirit. What does this phrase really mean? I believe Enoch provides an example. He walked with God and he was taken into Heaven. Today the Lord is raising up a generation of Christians who understand walking in the Spirit. This generation will become like Enoch: a generation who walks with God and is taken up into the presence of the Lord. Walking in the Spirit means walking in the awareness of His presence. This is the normal Christian life: learning to abide in Him, to live empowered by His strength. As you begin to experience this outpouring, you will become increasingly thirsty for His presence. As you learn to drink in His glory, you will begin to walk in the Spirit. Walk in the Spirit and you will not fulfill the lusts of the flesh.

Jesus used slightly different terminology in John chapter 15:

> *Abide in Me, and I in you. As the branch cannot bear fruit of itself, except it abide in the vine; no more can ye, except ye abide in Me. I am the vine, ye are the branches: he that abideth in Me, and I in him, the same bringeth forth much fruit, for without Me ye can do nothing* (John 15:4-5).

He tells us to abide in Him. This means learning to recognize His presence, to live in awareness of Him, and to live by His strength and not our own. This is the true life of victory. As we abide in Christ, our lives will begin to change. People will notice changes in you. They will see joy instead of depression and confidence rather than fear. Peace will rule, not stress and anxiety. You will begin to bear greater fruit. *"Herein is my Father glorified, that ye bear much fruit; so shall ye be My disciples"* (John 15:8).

The people you associate with will also be changed. Your family and friends will respond to the Lord because of His obvious effect on your life. Jesus will be glorified by the fruit that you bear. This is the result of life behind the veil. In that place, your life is changed, as well as the lives of everyone around you. A changed life is the ultimate goal of revival. In His presence we have no choice but to change. The more time that you spend behind the veil, the more you will change. When you step over to the other side, this life loses its attractions. God has more for you than this world can offer. He offers another world to explore and enjoy. Don't be distracted from the true joy we were intended to experience.

His presence is a place of security. If we learn to come into His presence and live there, our futures are filled with peace and confidence. The hopes and dreams that you have given up on or thrown away will begin to come back to you in the presence of God. Not only will your dreams return, but the power to make them come true will also begin to flow from Heaven into your life. Make a quality decision today. Let's press in to know the Lord. Let's not linger in the outer courts of worldliness and religion. Let's push into the Holy Place behind the veil, where a place of rest, joy, and peace waits for you. He is waiting for you. Let us draw near to Him, leaving the cares and attractions of the world behind. Another world awaits you—the spiritual world of the presence of God.

CHAPTER 6

The Transfer of the Anointing

"Then [the apostles] *laid their hands on them one by one, and they received the Holy Spirit"* (Acts 8:17 AMP).

One of the outstanding and most amazing characteristics of this present outpouring is how easily this anointing is transferred to others. From time to time in my Christian experience, I have seen the anointing minister through men and women to individuals. People would be healed and blessed, but the tangible anointing never seemed to stay. The anointing would be on the person and the ministry, and when that person left, the anointing was gone as well. This present outpouring is not like that. All who receive a touch from God and start to pursue His presence, making themselves available to Him, will begin to experience the flow of the anointing coming through them. The youngest of Christians can become powerful instruments through which God can flow. This present anointing makes Mark 16:17 make sense: "*These signs shall follow them that believe....*"

For example, during a recent high school outreach, two teenage girls shared their testimony with a large group of non-Christian high school students. As these girls shared what God had done for them, the Holy Spirit fell on the gathering. Many of the unsaved youths began to laugh uncontrollably. Some fell to the ground, totally intoxicated by the Holy Spirit. These two girls from our church had only recently been filled with this revival anointing. As they simply told their story, the anointing was transferred to the other teenagers who were attending the meetings.

The Bible is full of examples of the transfer of the anointing. Jesus had many unusual manifestations when the Holy Spirit touched people and changed their lives. One of the great examples is found in Luke:

And a woman having an issue of blood twelve years, which had spent all her living upon physicians, neither could be healed of any, came behind Him and touched the border of His garment: and immediately her issue of blood stanched. And Jesus said, "Who touched Me?" When all denied, Peter and they that were with him said, "Master, the multitude throng Thee and press Thee, and sayest Thou, 'Who touched Me?'" And Jesus said, "Somebody hath touched Me: for I perceive that virtue is gone out of Me." And when the woman saw that she was not hid, she came trembling, and falling down before Him, she declared unto Him before all the people for what cause she had touched Him, and how she was healed immediately. And He said unto her, "Daughter, be of good comfort: thy faith hath made thee whole; go in peace" (Luke 8:43-48).

In this passage, a woman who had an incurable medical condition came to Jesus. Jesus was unaware of this woman or her disease. She actually touched Jesus in secret because her condition made her unclean and touching Jesus could bring serious repercussions. When she touched Jesus, the anointing flowed from

Him into her. Jesus actually felt the power flow out of Him and asked, "Who touched me?" The disciples were confused by His statement because so many people were touching Him. He explained to them that someone had touched Him with the touch of faith, which made a demand on the anointing within Him. That anointing healed the woman's body.

Another example of the transfer of the anointing in the ministry of Jesus is found in Mark:

> *And He took the blind man by the hand, and led him out of the town; and when He had spit on his eyes, and had put His hands upon him, He asked him if he saw ought. And he looked up and said, "I see men as trees walking." After that He put His hands again upon his eyes, and had him look up: and he was restored, and saw every man clearly* (Mark 8:23-25).

In this passage, Jesus spit on a blind man's eyes. This practice was highly controversial and would have been considered unacceptable. I can just hear the Pharisees' complaints, "This spitting ministry has got to go. Turning water into wine, walking on water, talking to storms, and now spitting. We have got to put a stop to this fanatical behavior."

Regardless of what the religious people said, the blind man was healed. The anointing of God was transmitted to this man's body through Jesus' saliva. The tangible anointing touched his eyes and restored his vision. Many considered Jesus' ministry bizarre, but He always depended on the anointing to touch and change people's lives.

On the day of Pentecost, the 120 who were gathered in the upper room received the same anointing that was upon the ministry of Jesus (see Acts 2:1-4:43). The works that He did, they began to do also (see John 14:12). Signs and wonders were commonplace and many unusual miracles, including the transfer of the anointing, characterized the ministry of the apostles. One example is found in Acts 5:

> *And by the hands of the apostles were many signs and wonders wrought among the people; (and they were all with one accord in Solomon's porch. And the rest durst no man join himself to them: but the people magnified them. And believers were the more added to the Lord, multitudes both of men and women.) Insomuch that they brought forth the sick into the streets, and laid them on beds and couches, that at the least the shadow of Peter passing by might overshadow some of them. There came also a multitude out of the cities round about unto Jerusalem, bringing sick folks, and them which were vexed with unclean spirits: and they were healed every one* (Acts 5:12-16).

God used Peter in a very unusual way. Just the touch of his shadow healed people. There was nothing unusual about Peter's shadow except that it was a point of contact through which God transmitted the anointing. Just as the hem of Jesus' garment or His saliva on the blind man's eyes became a point contact to release the anointing, Peter's shadow became God's instrument to heal multitudes in the streets of Jerusalem.

Peter had another unusual experience while preaching at Cornelius' house:

> *While Peter yet spake these words, the Holy Ghost fell on all them which heard the word. And they of the circumcision which believed were astonished, as many as came with Peter, because that on the Gentiles also was poured out the gift of the Holy Ghost. For they heard them speak with tongues, and magnify God. Then answered Peter, "Can any man forbid water, that these should not be baptized, which have received the Holy Ghost as well as we?" And he commanded them to be baptized in the name of the Lord. Then prayed they him to tarry certain days* (Acts 10:44-48).

While Peter was preaching about Jesus, the presence of God fell on the people present at the meeting. They were filled with the Holy Ghost and spoke in other tongues. The Lord used words as the instrument to release the anointing. Peter was not able to finish his message or even to give an altar call. The Holy Spirit interrupted the meeting and holy chaos erupted in that house. This scene sounds strangely familiar. This manifestation sounds exactly like the current move of the Holy Ghost.

One final example can be seen in Acts 19:

And God wrought special miracles by the hands of Paul: so that from his body were brought unto the sick handkerchiefs or aprons, and the diseases departed from them, and the evil spirits went out of them (Acts 19:11-12).

Unusual miracles occurred through the ministry of Paul. Handkerchiefs or cloths that had touched Paul's body healed people who were sick or tormented by devils. The pieces of cloth carried Paul's anointing. Everyone they touched was healed and delivered from evil spirits. These pieces of cloth were not special. They became carriers of the anointing. The same anointing that was on Jesus came upon Paul when he was filled with the Spirit, and miracles began to follow his ministry.

This present outpouring is characterized by the transferability of the anointing. The anointing is transferred through words, through a touch, or just being close to someone full of the anointing. Videos, television broadcasts, teaching tapes, radio, and worship cd's can all carry this anointing. It is wonderful. God is spreading this move rapidly around the world. Today you can receive a touch from God. Get around the anointing. Attend revival meetings, watch videos, and listen to CDs; you will find yourself lost in the glory of God.

CHAPTER 7

Change—The Fruit of Revival

So repent (change your mind and purpose); turn around and return [to God], that your sins may be erased (blotted out, wiped clean), that times of refreshing (of recovering from the effects of heat, of reviving with fresh air) may come from the presence of the Lord (Acts 3:19 AMP).

B ut what good are all of these manifestations? Is there any fruit? This is one of the most common questions people have about the revival. Many have focused on the manifestations and not realized what is really happening to people. You may look at someone who is rolling on the floor in uncontrollable laughter and think that such behavior is not really necessary. When looking at the outside, you cannot see God's work. But when people are under the anointing, the Lord is working on their inside. They may be laughing, crying, or shaking on the outside, but on the inside they are being changed.

The greatest proof of the reality of this revival time is what the Lord did for me. I had been through some tough years in my ministry (1987-1992), and had lost the joy of serving the Lord. Our church had experienced the proverbial "building program from hell," which resulted in much financial chaos. The fallout had affected me more than I realized, and I battled depression and discouragement constantly. When I first experienced the awesome power of His presence and was filled with the joy of the Lord, all of this changed. It was as if I took off a coat of depression and put on a garment of praise and a mantle of joy. The fear of failure and calamity left me, and now confidence and joy continues to surge through my life.

Ezekiel identified the key element of revival:

> *Then will I sprinkle clean water upon you, and ye shall be clean: from all your filthiness, and from all your idols, will I cleanse you. A new heart also will I give you, and a new spirit will I put within you: and I will take away the stony heart out of your flesh, and I will give you an heart of flesh. And I will put my spirit within you, and cause you to walk in my statutes, and ye shall keep my judgments, and do them (Ezekiel 36:25-27).*

The most important manifestation in this revival is unseen to the natural eye. It is the change in people's hearts. Cold hearts are being fired with the passion of first love for Jesus. Hard hearts are being softened and molded by the Potter's hands. Rebellious hearts are broken and changed into humble and submissive hearts. Depressed hearts are comforted and filled with the joy of His presence and service. The Lord is doing surgery on people, and their lives will never be the same.

Some pastor friends of ours from years back came to visit us while Rodney Howard-Browne was at our church. We had known them for over 20 years. They had been a major influence in our lives as new Christians. Little did we realize, after all these years, that our stories were the same. Burned-out and bummed-out, their circumstances were different, but their story sounded all too familiar. We watched in amazement as once again the Holy Spirit operated like no other. It was wonderful to see them change as they sat in the services.

The church was in the second week of the revival, and Brother Rodney decided to hold a huge baptism that Friday night. So, when Friday night came, our church was transformed into a giant burial ground—people were dying to their flesh and coming alive in Christ. We laid plastic everywhere; ushers with mops and towels ran around assisting the newly birthed. What a night! I'll never forget it! Hundreds and hundreds went down into the water grave that night and came out with the power of God. Usually about seven people or so would go into the pool and you would hear Brother Rodney say, "Raise your hands and let the power of God touch you. *Fill*!" Then they had to be fished out of the pool, and the ushers would carry them and lay them out on the plastic. We were overcome with weeping as we watched our church members go down into that pool, where God deeply touched and transformed them.

Our pastor friends were also baptized. I saw the wife go down into the water, and watched the ushers fish her out of the pool, pass her from usher to usher, and finally lay her down with all the others. All she can remember about that night is the usher saying, "We have another carry out!"

They went home that week and put up a new sign outside their church: Under New Management. The church members now call the pastor's wife "Smiley." Oh, the goodness of God! Where would we be if it hadn't been for Him? Don't tell me that this isn't real; it's too late. The pastor's wife went back to her church and preached from John chapter 9, the story of Jesus healing the blind man. When questioned by the religious leaders, the man said, *"One thing I know: that though I was blind, now I see"* (John 9:25 NKJV). Oh, to be that simple again. Let's allow the Holy Spirit back into our lives. Let's become like children again.

Can we stop being so complicated? I don't know how, and I don't have all the questions answered. All I know is that I once was blind, but now I see.

Some people do not understand the drunken behavior that accompanies the anointing of the Holy Spirit. It may seem difficult to look beyond the outward behavior and comprehend the internal reality. A homeless man came to one of our meetings and saw people laughing and drunk in the Holy Ghost. He didn't know what was happening, but he knew a good party when he saw one, so he got into the prayer line. Touched by God, he found himself on the floor, full of the joy of the Lord. What happened next is the fruit of revival.

This man was scheduled to have heart surgery later that week. He checked into the hospital, and they began to run tests on him. One of the doctors asked him what he had been doing lately. The doctor said that, unexplainably, he had a brand-new heart. The man told the doctor that he had had no medical treatment, but that he had gone to church and that a drunken pastor had prayed for him. When this man received prayer, all the natural mind could see was a homeless drunk rolling on the floor. Little did anyone know that more than laughter was taking place on the inside. The Lord had given him a brand-new heart, as well as joy unspeakable and full of glory.

My wife's sister had been foster-parenting for a few years, hoping to adopt the babies placed in her home. After she took care of two sisters for two years, the state gave the children back to their birth mother. Of course, my sister-in-law was devastated. In a few months the state gave her two more little girls. As she tried again to adopt her new foster children, she struggled with anxiety. Then she came to some revival meetings at our church and was tremendously touched. She received the joy of the Lord again. Her life would never be the same. And she was, shortly afterward, permitted to adopt the girls.

True joy comes from a changed heart. When you experience repentance, you have peace with God and peace with your family and friends. True joy springs from this pure and holy atmosphere. Critics of joy and laughter only look skin deep. They have eyes to see but they cannot (see Matt. 13:15-16). We must push beyond the surface into the heart of man. In a man's heart is where revival begins.

You can never judge a move of God by outward circumstances. You must evaluate the fruit. I say to the critics, look at the fruit. Ask the rebellious teenager who is now humble and full of the love of Jesus. Ask the homeless couple who now have jobs and a place to live. Ask the teenager from the mental institution about the peace and love that he has found in the Lord. Ask the wife whose husband finally got saved after years of marriage problems. Ask the cancer patients who have been healed. Ask the heart patient with a new heart.

Remember in John chapter 9 the blind man who was healed and interrogated by the Pharisees. They were asking who Jesus was. The man said:

> *Why, this is a marvelous thing, that you do not know where He is from; yet He has opened my eyes! Now we know that God does not hear sinners; but if anyone is a worshiper of God and does His will, He hears him. Since the world began it has been unheard of that anyone opened the eyes of one who was born blind. If this Man were not from God, He could do nothing* (John 9:30-33 NKJV).

Here are a few of the testimonies that have come pouring into our church:

⊱ It was on February 13, 1995, when I was first able to surrender; to yield to His anointing. I've been pressing in for 16 months now. I've been coming to church every time the doors are open. I've been in prayer lines every time I could stand and get to them. As a result, I've been set free through His joy and His love after living 38 years of my life in fear and torment. I was emotionally paralyzed, very limited in my ability to function outside of "safety zones" that I created for myself. I loved the Lord very much; I sang and worshipped and read the Word, but I kept Him at a safe distance until recently. The Lord has used His Word and His Holy Spirit to comfort me. The Lord spoke to my heart, "*Taste and see that the Lord is good.*" I was valuable to the Lord. He loved me, He would care for me, and He would never leave me. He could turn my mourning into dancing. He could take all the fear and destruction that I had in my soul and turn me around as a sign and a wonder of His great love and mercy. I've pressed in and found that joy unspeakable—now I laugh; I shout, and I dance like an exuberant child, secure in the knowledge of her daddy's love. As I dance, I am freed; I am filled with joy and love for my Father. Nothing else really matters but being filled with the Holy Spirit and sharing this love with others.

⮘ Two years ago, I went to the doctor because I felt a pain in my heart. I was diagnosed with Mitral Prolaps and a heart murmur. The doctor told me that I was born with this condition and that there was no cure. My heart would start beating abnormally, and I would feel like I couldn't breathe. When I found out, the first thing that I did was pray to God for healing. I went to the doctor six months after I had stopped taking my medication. I told him that I believed God would heal me. The doctor said that things were looking good, but that I should come back in one year. At church one night, I felt God touch me, and I believed that this was the day God was going to heal my heart. Norman Robertson was the guest speaker, and he said that someone in the audience was being healed of a problem in their heart. I screamed from the deepest part of my soul because I knew it was me! I went back to the doctor for my annual checkup. After running tests, he said that the results were inaccurate because my heart appeared normal. He redid the tests and called me two days later to tell me that nothing was wrong with my heart. He discharged me and agreed that only God could have done this.

∞ I found a lump in my body and went to a doctor to have it checked. After two days of testing (72 CAT scans, x-rays, blood work and numerous doctor's exams), I was told that I had a massive tumor. The doctors gave me no hope. They said that radiation and chemotherapy would not work on my type of tumor and that I should gather my friends and family together because I would need their support. Their opinion was that I had only a couple of months to live. Two and a half years later, I'm still standing on God's Word! I have not been incapacitated in any way. I have been enjoying the river of God's anointing which brings me life and daily sustains me.

∞ Several years ago, I discovered a growth on my body. I prayed about it and believed that God would heal me, but from time to time I considered going to a doctor. One night at church, several people were called up to the front for prayer. While I was at the altar, I fell into a trance and began laughing and singing and praying. I knew I had been touched by God but was not sure exactly what had happened. The next day, while taking a shower, I discovered that the growth was totally gone. A real, physical manifestation of God's outpouring has happened in my life!

CHAPTER 8

Glimpses of His Glory

This act in Cana of Galilee was the first sign Jesus gave, the first glimpse of His glory. And His disciples believed in Him (John 2:11 TM).

The first miracle that Jesus performed was very interesting and gives us the first glimpse of the glory of God coming through the ministry of Jesus. Jesus, a guest at a wedding, performed an unnecessary miracle. They were running out of wine, so Jesus turned some water into wine. This was His first miracle. No one's life was in jeopardy, and the people did not really need any more wine. Jesus was just being a blessing.

The Word of God gives us glimpses of the ministry of the Holy Spirit. These glimpses come in the form of metaphors, such as a cloud, oil, wind, rain, fire, a river, and wine. These word pictures help us relate to the awesome person of the Holy Spirit. He is truly a person and is God Himself. He deserves our praise and adoration just as much as the Father and the Son. Unfortunately, many people have struggled to understand and relate to the Holy Spirit. This present outpouring has a unique personality and can be characterized by many of these word pictures found throughout the Word of God. The anointing of the Holy Spirit is not an experience, and it is more than just speaking in tongues. This anointing brings us into a vast, bottomless realm of the glory of God. As we yield to Him, we can explore the incredible universe of the presence of God.

One glimpse into this realm is found in the cloud of glory, which is most vividly recorded in Second Chronicles:

> *Indeed it came to pass, when the trumpeters and singers were as one, to make one sound to be heard in praising and thanking the Lord, and when they lifted up their voice with the trumpets and cymbals and instruments of music, and praised the Lord, saying: "For He is good, for His mercy endures forever," that the house, the house of the Lord, was filled with a cloud, so that the priests could not continue ministering because of the cloud; for the glory of the Lord filled the house of God* (2 Chronicles 5:13-14 NKJV).

In this passage of Scripture, the cloud of glory manifested visibly during the dedication of Solomon's temple. The presence was so strong that no one could stand; everyone was lying on the floor under the anointing of the Holy Spirit. This cloud appears throughout the Bible. It led the children of Israel for 40 years in the wilderness. It appeared on the Mount of Transfiguration with Jesus, Moses, and Elijah.

This cloud illustrates one of the vital ministries of the Holy Spirit. He is our protection and insulation. When Moses and the children of Israel first left Egypt, Pharaoh and the Egyptian army pursued them. The cloud, which had been in front of the children of Israel, moved behind them. The presence of the Lord shielded them from the Egyptians. In the same way, we need His tangible anointing to protect us from the onslaughts that come against us. We live in a changing world filled with danger: danger from criminals, terrorists, rapidly-changing weather patterns, earthquakes, storms, and many other things. There also seems to be a rising tide of persecution, especially against the manifestation of the power of God. This outpouring of the Holy Spirit provides insulation and protection from all of these dangers. He becomes like a blanket, protecting us from all of the emotional and physical attacks that come against us.

Another glimpse into the person of the Holy Spirit is the oil of gladness. Hebrews says,

> *But unto the Son He saith, "Thy throne, O God, is for ever and ever: a sceptre of righteousness is the sceptre of thy kingdom. Thou hast loved righteousness, and hated iniquity; therefore God, even thy God, hath anointed thee with the oil of gladness above thy fellows"* (Hebrews 1:8-9).

The anointing, throughout the Scriptures, was characterized by oil. The prophets, priests, and kings were anointed with oil when they began their ministries. In the New Testament, we are directed to pray for the sick and anoint them with oil.

The anointing is the equipment given to us by the Holy Spirit to do the tasks set before us. In Luke 24:49, the Lord told us to wait for the Holy Spirit until we are clothed (equipped) with power from on high. Just as the Old Testament leaders were anointed with oil and with the Holy Spirit, we receive a tangible anointing that gives us everything we need to touch this world for Jesus.

Just before I experienced this present revival anointing, I had become very weary in the work of the Lord. The joy of ministering to people had somehow slipped away from me. When I began my ministry, everything was fresh and exciting. But as time went on, it became more of a job and less enjoyable. When I was touched by this new anointing, I experienced two immediate changes. First, I received new equipment, new supernatural abilities in my ministry. Second, the ministry became fun again. Now I understand the oil of gladness. His anointing equips us for our jobs and fills our hearts with joy as we work. Open your heart to this fresh outpouring. Let Him fill you with the oil of gladness. Your greatest joy will become pouring out His oil so that others can receive it as well.

The wind is an awesome picture of the ministry of the Holy Spirit. The first Sunday that our church entered into revival, I felt wind blowing in our sanctuary.

> *And when the day of Pentecost was fully come, they were all with one accord in one place. And suddenly there came a sound from heaven as of a rushing mighty wind, and it filled all the house where they were sitting* (Acts 2:1-2).

As we opened up to the move of God that first Sunday, hundreds of people were touched powerfully by the Holy Spirit. Many of the individuals shared about being refreshed by the touch of God. They were being strengthened spiritually, emotionally, and physically. At this writing, more than fourteen years have passed since that initial outpouring in our church. This refreshing revival has lasted and increased as thousands have been touched by God's wind in our church.

In Acts 3:19, Peter said that the Lord would send times of refreshing through His presence. The Amplified Bible expands refreshing as, *"recovering from the effects of heat"* and *"reviving with fresh air."* The Body of Christ has a constant need of refreshing. This awesome outpouring of God is like a cool breeze on a hot summer's day. God's wind is blowing throughout the earth today. Maybe you feel tired and beat up. Step into the wind of God, and He will strengthen and refresh you with His awesome presence.

In the Book of Joel we get another glimpse into the Holy Spirit:

> *Be glad then, you children of Zion, and rejoice in the Lord your God; for He has given you the former rain faithfully, and He will cause the rain to come down for you—the former rain, and the latter rain in the first month. The threshing floors shall be full of wheat, and the vats shall overflow with new wine and oil* (Joel 2:23-24 NKJV).

In this passage, Joel talks about the former and latter rain in Israel. This rain was the key to the prosperity of the land. The Lord would send two seasons of rain that caused the crops in Israel to be the best in the world. Peter preached about this on the day of Pentecost (see Acts 2:16-21). He preached that the Pentecostal outpouring was the fulfillment of Joel's prophecy. Just as the rain brought growth and blessing to Israel, this spiritual rain brings blessing and growth to our lives today.

The rain of the Holy Spirit is falling throughout the earth today. Cathedral of Praise in Manila, Philippines, pastored by David Sumrall, has been powerfully touched by this current outpouring. Recently, I was in one of their meetings when it started to rain outside. This was an answer to prayer because the nation was experiencing a drought. As the natural rain pounded on the roof, the spiritual rain began to fall on the congregation. Pastor Sumrall began to prophesy, "It's raining; the tough times are over."

Just as the physical rain brought blessing to the land, the spiritual rain brought blessing to the people. When the rain comes, everything begins to break out into new life. From that day, Cathedral of Praise has experienced tremendous growth: spiritual growth for the members, financial growth for the ministry, and numerical growth in the congregation. When the rain begins to fall, new life is everywhere. Get ready, I hear the sound of an abundance of rain coming toward you.

Another awesome depiction of the Holy Spirit is fire. The fire of God fell from Heaven many times in Scripture. We see the fire in Moses' burning bush, in the pillar of fire, in the fire that consumed Elijah's sacrifice, in the fire that fell at the dedication of Solomon's temple, and in the tongues of fire that rested on the believers on the day of Pentecost.

And there appeared unto them cloven tongues like as of fire, and it sat upon each of them. And they were all filled with the Holy Ghost, and began to speak with other tongues, as the Spirit gave them utterance (Acts 2:3-4).

The fire depicts another awesome facet of the ministry of the Holy Spirit. It speaks to us of the purifying work of the Holy Ghost. When you spend time in His presence, you are convicted of the sin and compromise in your life. You begin to lose your taste for the things of this world. The more time you spend in His presence, the more you will change. Worldliness will become a thing of the past in your life.

Many people have said that this revival is just about laughing, that it is emotional and shallow. But those who feel this way have never experienced the fiery touch of God upon their lives. This outpouring, which is the cleansing fire of God falling from Heaven, is holy and very serious. A young man in our church got enough fire in his life to take on the public high schools in our city. Since being touched, he has boldly taught a salvation message, holding rallies at schools. Another man felt called to go into the housing developments, fill our church buses with children, and hold services for them. My brother-in-law, a successful man who owned his own business, felt the call of God to pioneer a church in his city. He named it Joy Fellowship.

Another example of the presence of God is found in Revelation:

And he shewed me a pure river of water of life, clear as crystal, proceeding out of the throne of God and of the Lamb. In the midst of the street of it, and on either side of the river, was there the tree of life, which bare twelve manner of fruits, and yielded her fruit every month: and the leaves of the tree were for the healing of the nations (Revelation 22:1-2).

This presents the Holy Spirit as the river that flows from the throne of God. Everywhere this river goes, it brings life as a result. This river of God is bringing healing to the nations. Jesus said that anyone who was thirsty could come to Him and drink. Then, rivers of living water would flow out of their spirits (see John 7:37-39). Everyone who is touched by this revival and yields to this anointing becomes a channel for revival. They become a river bank for the glory of God. If you are thirsty, you can come and drink from His presence. As you drink, His love, joy and peace will fill you. As you continue to drink, the anointing will flow out of you to touch others. Out of your belly will flow rivers of living water. As you learn to flow in this river of God, you will become a blessing to others. Life will continually flow out of you. The people you touch will begin to experience the life that flows from Jesus, who is seated on the throne of God.

Finally, Jesus compared a fresh move of the Holy Spirit to new wine:

And no man putteth new wine into old bottles: else the new wine doth burst the bottles, and the wine is spilled, and the bottles will be marred: but new wine must be put into new bottles (Mark 2:22).

Jesus compared a fresh move of the Holy Spirit to new wine. The reason Jesus used wine as an illustration is because it makes you drunk. When you begin to drink the new wine of the Holy Spirit, you become intoxicated with the glory of God.

In our city, New Orleans, people from all over the world come to visit Bourbon Street. It's known for its "big easy" attitude—drunkenness, homosexuals dressed in drag, strippers, and many other venues for sin. After this anointing touched our lives, we felt compelled to open a church there. In the natural, this is an impossible task. The rent alone costs $5,000 a month! But we found a place (dead center on Bourbon Street), and we now have an outreach named Cafe Joel. Cafe Joel has brought the new wine to Bourbon Street, touching hundreds of lives. This is what lost people are looking for—the touch of God!

What does it mean to be drunk in the spirit? It means to become more aware of the presence of God and less aware of this natural world. When we press into the realm of God, the things of this earth grow strangely dim. Drinking the new wine fills us with the awareness of God. This is what Peter called *"joy unspeakable and full of glory"* (1 Pet. 1:8).

In the initial Pentecostal outpouring, the 120 believers were full of the Holy Spirit and appeared to be drunk. Their outrageous behavior attracted a crowd of thousands of people. They were loud and full of joy and laughter. The observers could come up with only one explanation: these people must be drunk (see Acts 2:13). But Peter said, *"These are not drunken as ye suppose, but this is that which was spoken by the prophet Joel"* (Acts 2:15-16). Peter attributed the drunken behavior to the outpouring of the Holy Spirit. Today thousands of people are learning to drink the new wine. They are tired of symbolic religion. They are hungry for reality.

These pictures of the Holy Spirit give us glimpses into reality. They provide windows into the world of the supernatural. Just as when Jesus turned the water into wine and the disciples saw a glimpse of His glory, today the Holy Spirit outpouring is giving us a wonderful taste of the powers of the world to come.

CHAPTER 9

The Spirit of Truth

But when the Comforter is come, whom I will send unto you from the Father, even the Spirit of Truth, which proceedeth from the Father, He shall testify of Me (John 15:26).

P eople today are hungry for what is real. They are tired of forms, programs, and hype. Basically, religion has run its course and has failed miserably. Reality can be found only in the presence of God. Jesus said, "*But when the Comforter is come, whom I will send unto you from the Father, even the Spirit of Truth, which proceedeth from the Father, he shall testify of me*" (John 15:26). Jesus addressed our hunger for reality when He taught His followers about the Holy Spirit. He said that when the Holy Spirit comes, He will lead us into all truth. This truth is more than just facts or right information. Right information is taught by many people who have no concept of the presence of God or of the reality of the Holy Spirit.

Greek scholar Dr. Spiros Zodhiates defines the Greek word for truth, *aletheia*, as "the unveiled reality lying at the basis of and agreeing with an appearance; the manifested or veritable essence of a matter; the reality pertaining to appearance."[1] This is the kind of truth that Jesus taught about. He was telling us that the Holy Spirit would come and make the Word of God, His presence, Jesus, the Heavenly Father, and all of the things of God, real in our lives. This outpouring of the Holy Spirit brings us from philosophy into reality. Man truly hungers for the glory of God.

In one of our services, my daughter Grace, who was six years old at the time, was mightily touched by the presence of the Lord. Actually, it was the final meeting of a three-week revival at our church, conducted by Rodney Howard-Browne. Toward the end of the service, during the salvation altar call, the power of God fell upon Grace. She began to laugh, cry, shake, and make all sorts of noises. After the altar call was completed, Brother Rodney called Grace to the platform. She started to move toward the platform but fell to the ground, totally intoxicated by the Holy Spirit. She was carried to the platform where she shook uncontrollably for approximately 30 minutes. After she was able to walk, Brother Rodney had some ministers come forward for prayer. He had Grace lay hands on each one, and they were all knocked to the floor by the power of God. Since that night, there has been a change in Grace. She is very sensitive to God's presence and is filled with a brand-new joy. She always talks about people being "hit with the joy."

This reality of God is the hope for the next generation. Formulas, programs, philosophy, and regulations are not enough to change the lives of our children. Only the power of God can solve the complicated problems of our world today.

This truth of the reality of God versus symbolic religion, shows up throughout the ministry of Jesus. One example is found in John chapter 4:

> *But the hour cometh, and now is, when the true wor-shippers shall worship the Father in spirit and in truth: for the Father seeketh such to worship him. God is a Spirit: and they that worship him must worship him in spirit and in truth* (John 4:23-24).

Jesus was speaking to the Samaritan woman about true worship. She was talking about religion and certain practices, and Jesus told her about worshiping in spirit and reality. Most so-called worship comes just from our lips and our heads. But true worship comes passionately from our hearts. This true worship brings us into the reality of the presence of God.

Jesus also spoke of the Spirit of Truth when He said, "*But when the Comforter is come, whom I will send unto you from the Father, even the Spirit of Truth, which proceedeth from the Father, he shall testify of Me*" (John 15:26). In this passage, Jesus told the disciples that the Holy Spirit would speak to them about Him. One of the awesome functions of the Holy Spirit is to make Jesus come alive to us.

When we are filled with His presence, we begin to see how wonderful Jesus is. The more we are filled with the anointing, the more in love with Jesus we become. He speaks to us about the death and resurrection of Jesus. He talks to us about Jesus being exalted above every name and being glorified on the throne. He speaks to us about the powerful name of Jesus. He also reminds us of the soon return of our Lord. The Spirit of Truth constantly makes Jesus alive and personal in our lives.

Jesus also talks about the Spirit of Truth in John chapter 16:

> *Howbeit when He, the Spirit of Truth, is come, He will guide you into all truth: for He shall not speak of Himself; but whatsoever He shall hear, that shall He*

speak: and He will shew you things to come (John 16:13).

In this passage, Jesus says that the Holy Spirit talks to us about things to come. In the presence of the Lord, we begin to see the plans of God. He fills our hearts with His visions and dreams for our lives. He adjusts the desires of our hearts until we are on fire with His plans. He pours out His compassion within us, urging us on to reach those He wants us to touch.

The Spirit of Truth, the Holy Spirit, has become my friend. I am learning to trust Him and to depend on Him for everything. The reality of His touch has made life fun again. He has made church fun again. Make a decision today that you will never settle for forms and programs again. You will settle for nothing less than the real. You will press through into the real, into the glory of God.

ENDNOTE

1. Spiros Zodhiates, *The Complete Word Study Dictionary: New Testament,* second edition. (Chattanooga, TN: AMG Publishers, 1993).

CHAPTER 10

Call to the Nations

All the ends of the world shall remember and turn to the Lord, and all the families of the nations shall worship before You (Psalm 22:27 NKJV).

One of the great prophecies from the Old Testament began to be fulfilled on the day of Pentecost. Peter preached from Joel, which said that in the last days God would pour out of His Spirit on all flesh (see Joel 2:28; Acts 2:17). When the Holy Spirit fell on the day of Pentecost, that prophecy began to be fulfilled. Thousands and thousands were saved after the initial outpouring of the Holy Spirit. Over the years, however, the Church fell into religion and tradition, and the power of the Holy Spirit became a thing of the past.

Throughout history various outpourings and revivals have touched many nations and regions. In this century, the Pentecostal outpouring has touched most of the world. Many believe that this present move of the Holy Spirit could be the final fulfillment of God's promise that He will pour out His Spirit on all flesh. This revival has spread rapidly over the past few years. The United States, Canada, Central and South America, the United Kingdom, Scandinavia and much of Europe have been touched mightily by this revival. Parts of Africa, Asia, and Australia have also seen a new wind blow across the land.

Expectancy of last day revival seems to be surging throughout the Church. The Lord has restored a desire for a calling to the nations in my heart. I have recently conducted revival meetings in various nations and have been amazed at the hunger and receptivity of the people. God's glory is flooding the earth.

I want to share with you one experience that I have had with revival in the nations. My good friend, David Sumrall, contacted me shortly after my visitation of the Holy Spirit. David pastors in Manila, Philippines, where I have ministered with him over the years. David heard that I was laughing, so he gave me a call. He wanted to know what was going on. I believe David was surprised because he had known me for years and had seen that I stayed away from the fads that blow through the Church. I tried to share with him what had happened to me, and I began to cry, which is totally out of character for me. David's curiosity was aroused, so he came to visit me for three days at my home in New Orleans. He had many questions about the revival, and we had numerous discussions during that time. At the end of his stay, our ministers prayed for him, and David fell under the power of God and began to laugh (this was a first).

When David returned to his church, he shared with his ministers what had happened. After some initial resistance, his staff opened up and received the mighty move of God. David called and asked me to come to Manila that week. I was able to arrange for the trip, and when I arrived, I found his staff totally saturated in the glory of God. I ministered in their staff meeting that Friday, and the place was filled with joy unspeakable. The entire staff (75 pastors) was on the floor in the presence of the Lord. I conducted services in the church for five days, and the glory of God moved powerfully. The church seemed to be basking in liquid joy. Thousands of people were totally beside themselves in holy pandemonium. Cathedral of Praise is a church of more than 20,000 members. They have held daily meetings for over one year. Pastors and ministers from all over the Philippines and Asia have visited this church and have been touched by revival. Sustained revival has spread to many locations as a result.

One of the great desires of my heart has been to be involved in world missions. As I got older and went through tough ministry years, I thought that dream would never happen. Not only has my dream been fulfilled, but my wildest expectations have been surpassed just by that one meeting in the Philippines. What a humbling experience to be used in the revival. What an honor to be a co-laborer with the Holy Spirit. The Bible says that the whole earth will be covered with the glory of the Lord. That is literally being fulfilled before our very eyes. The nations are being swept into the flow of revival.

As I have recently spent more time in meetings and in the presence of the Lord, I feel an urgency growing in my heart. There is not much time. The coming of the Lord is closer than many of us think. If you have ever felt that you would do something for the Lord, the time of waiting is over. It is time for all of us to get into the river of God. It is time to launch out into the deep. It is time to go to the nations.

And the Spirit and the bride say "Come." And let him that heareth say, "Come." And let him that is athirst come. And whosoever will, let him take of the water of life freely (Revelation 22:17).

Section Two

Proclaiming the Glory of God

Introduction

Several years ago, I was preaching about God's purpose for creation when I felt that still small voice inside disagreeing with my message. Nothing is quite as alarming as being corrected by the Lord in the midst of preaching. I can remember exactly where I was at the time, David Sumrall's Cathedral of Praise in Manila, Philippines. After the service, I began to search the Scriptures about the purpose for creation. The more I searched, the more I was confronted with the glory of God. Everything was created to display and magnify God's glory. Paul said it like this:

> *For since the creation of the world His invisible attributes are clearly seen, being understood by the things that are made, even His eternal power and Godhead, so that they are without excuse* (Romans 1:20 NKJV).

Suddenly, everywhere I looked I saw the display of His glory. I saw His power and wisdom in creation, His love and grace in the person of Jesus, His wisdom and mercy in His plan of redemption, His joy in the outpourings of His presence, His counsel in the Word of God. Not only that, but I saw His plan revealed in the outpourings of history and His sovereignty revealed in the catastrophes and blessings of life. How unsearchable are His ways; how deep is His wisdom (see Rom. 11:33).

Jonathan Edwards preached about the purpose for creation in his book, *The End For Which God Created the Earth*. Edwards' teaching on the glory of God revealed in all things has significantly impacted my life and my pursuit of the glory of the Lord. He wrote:

> In the creature's knowing, esteeming, loving, rejoicing in, and praising God, the glory of God is both exhibited and acknowledged; His fullness is received and returned. Here is both emanation and remanation. The refulgence shines upon and into the creature and is reflected back to the luminary. The beams of Glory come from God, and are something of God, and are refunded back again to their original. So that the whole is of God, and God is the beginning, middle and end in this affair.[1]

The bottom line is this: I was created to enjoy God. As the Lord becomes real to me, my joy increases. My joy, my experience of God, brings glory to the Lord. I was created to glorify God by enjoying Him forever. Part of His joy is proclaiming His glory to the nations. As my cup is full and overflows, it overflows in ministry to the hurting people of the world.

In this second section of *The Unseen World of the Holy Spirit*, you will come with me on my journey in search of the joy that comes from proclaiming His goodness to the world. I pray that you will be captured by His glory in these pages and that you will taste His unspeakable joy, which He poured out for us in the person of the Holy Spirit.

ENDNOTE

1. Jonathan Edwards, *The End For Which God Created the Earth The Works of Jonathan Edwards Volume # 1*, (Banner of Truth, 1998): 120.

PART 1

Living Off of the Invisible God

CHAPTER I

Joseph's Multicolored, Invisible Coat

Now Israel [Jacob] loved Joseph more than all his children, because he was the son of his old age. Also he made him a tunic of many colors. But when his brothers saw that their father loved him more than all his brothers, they hated him and could not speak peaceably to him (Genesis 37:3-4 NKJV).

I n our modern society, it is not politically correct to say that a father loves one son more than the others. However, God wrote down this statement about Jacob and Joseph in His book. Some Bible commentaries actually criticize Jacob for showing partiality to his younger son. But the fact is, this story of Jacob and Joseph is a picture of how our heavenly Father feels about us.

From the day Joseph was born, he was chosen. His father loved him the first day he looked at him. He knew he was special, and he loved him. In the same way, our heavenly Father places His love upon us and blesses us with all spiritual blessings in the heavenly places in Christ Jesus. I was chosen as the son of His love before the foundation of the world. He loved me before He even created the world. He had me in mind from eternity (see Eph. 1:2-4). The Word of God says that I was engraved on His hand. I, Frank Bailey, was engraved on the hand of almighty God from eternity! For this reason, I know that He loves me with an everlasting love. He is drawing me with the cords of His love. Though I have not seen Him with my natural eyes, He has revealed His love to me through the person of the Holy Ghost. I am His son, a son of God. That is the story of Joseph.

Only two kinds of people exist in the world: the sons of God and the sons of the devil (see 1 Thess. 5:5). Jesus and Paul both taught this. In Colossians 3:6, Paul wrote that God's wrath comes upon *"the children of disobedience,"* and in Colossians 1:13, he wrote that God *"hath delivered us from the power of darkness, and hath translated us into the kingdom of his dear Son."* Can you imagine how horrifying it would be if satan walked into your room? The worst horror movie wouldn't even depict how terrible it would be. We can't even imagine his ugliness, his depraved nature, his arrogance, or his utter sinfulness. To be the son of the devil would be infinitely worse than just seeing him. His nature would be your nature.

Thank God that, as born-again Christians, we have been delivered from the kingdom of darkness and are no longer children of the devil. When we surrender our lives to God, we are translated into the kingdom of His beloved Son, born from above by His Spirit. The Spirit of adoption comes to live inside each born-again Christian, and we become children of God. I feel as if I am God's favorite son, and He loves me more than anyone else. But, actually, He can do that for everybody. He can love you more than anybody else. You can be His favorite. I don't understand exactly how it works, but He does.

The Book of Genesis tells us that Jacob loved his son Joseph more than all the rest of his children because Joseph was the son of his old age, and Jacob honored him with a coat of many colors. That physical coat was a picture of the anointing of God that was being placed upon Joseph's life.

God gave me a coat, too. He loved me so much that He said, "Son, I have a coat that I want you to wear. Would you wear this coat to honor Me? I prepared it just for you, and no one else has one like it." This coat, my friends, is the anointing of the Holy Spirit. It is the coat the Lord gives to all of His children.

When my Father gave me my coat, He warned me, "People might like it for a while, but it's going to go out of style. Would you wear it anyway in honor of Me, this coat of many colors? People may misunderstand you if you wear it, but would you wear it anyway? People will think you're wearing it because you're arrogant and proud. But, actually you're going to wear it out of respect for Me."

When Joseph's father gave him the coat of many colors, he faced the same questions. "Joseph, will you wear my coat everywhere you go?" Jacob might have asked. "Will you even wear it when you're out there rubbing shoulders with the children of disobedience, or with deceitful brethren?" Jacob must have known that Joseph would be misunderstood because of the coat he wore.

The picture of a new coat coming upon a chosen son of God reminds me of the New Testament story of blind Bartimaeus (see Mark 10:46-52). Sitting by the side of the road, he shook his little cup, a beggar living off of people's offerings. Bartimaeus depended on man. It was as though he was on welfare, and he couldn't get by on his own and live a normal life. One day, Bartimaeus heard that Jesus of Nazareth was passing by. In that moment, he threw off his old beggar's coat (see Mark 10:50). He was about to get a new one. He was about to step into the supernatural world and experience the power of the other side. He was about to get a glimpse of the invisible God. In an instant, Bartimaeus was healed.

Are you willing to throw off that old coat, to throw off your old way of living, your old pride, motives, sins, lusts, and offenses? Are you ready to just throw it off? Get rid of it! Be proud to wear the coat that your Father made for you. The coat of the Holy Ghost is a coat of miracles, a coat of the supernatural. You can wear it every day of your life. This is how Joseph was able to live the life that was planned for him. As he stood on the edge of his destiny, Joseph had no idea what trials he would face. Joseph didn't know that wearing this coat would make him so unpopular. He was just naïve enough to think that everybody would like it.

But sometimes the anointing does not make you popular. When God touched me in a supernatural way in 1994, I felt the Lord put the coat of glory on me. And, like Joseph, I was naïve enough to think that all of my friends, many of whom were well-known in Christian circles, would be happy about this new coat that I had received. Instead, I could give you a list of people from "Who's Who" in the Christian world who have rebuked me for my coat. But, I am wearing it anyway. Glory to God!

After Joseph received the coat from his father, he had two dreams. In these dreams, described in Genesis 37:7-9, Joseph's brothers and parents bowed down to him. When you put on the awesome coat of the Holy Ghost, suddenly you find yourself in the world of the supernatural. Just like Bartimaeus, you begin to experience new things. Under the anointing, you may lie on the floor and suddenly find yourself in another world, in the place of Jacob's ladder, in the place of visions and dreams. You see and hear things that you've never seen or heard before. The Word of God starts to become alive inside you and prophecy bubbles up within you. Miracles will flow from your hands. Strange and unusual tongues will well up out of your belly. This is the supernatural realm.

God brought Joseph into this supernatural realm in order to take him into his destiny. The invisible God was equipping Joseph with all that he would need for his journey. Joseph couldn't get by just on his natural strength, in the same way that you and I can't get by on simplistic Christian-empowerment slogans. Slogans don't work in prison, my friends. You need the power of God. Cute little Christian phrases won't make it. You need the supernatural. You need to live in the land of visions and dreams. You need to put on that invisible coat, the anointing of the Holy Spirit.

> *So it came to pass, when Joseph had come to his brothers, that they stripped Joseph of his tunic, the tunic of many colors that was on him* (Genesis 37:23 NKJV).

At the age of 17, Joseph's father sent him to check on his brothers. Offended by Joseph's visions and dreams, and by the love that flowed to him from their father, Joseph's brothers stripped him of the outward sign. But no one could take away his real coat. Wrapped in that invisible coat, Joseph could walk protected, with almighty God as his constant companion.

> *Then they took him and cast him into a pit. And the pit was empty; there was no water in it....So Judah said to his brothers, "What profit is there if we kill our brother and conceal his blood? Come and let us sell him to the Ishmaelites, and let not our hand be upon him, for he is our brother and our flesh." And his brothers listened* (Genesis 37:24;26-27 NKJV).

After they threw Joseph into the pit, neither they nor Joseph had any idea what was about to happen. His brothers planned to kill him, but instead they spared him and sold him into slavery. In order to fulfill His plan, God sent Joseph ahead of his brothers to be their deliverer. God used the very ones who despised and spoke evil of Joseph to send him on his way to Egypt.

Joseph needed the supernatural where he was going. When God gave Joseph the invisible coat of the anointing, He knew that he was going to be sold into slavery and taken to Egypt. At the tender age of 17, Joseph needed something supernatural to sustain him. In the same way, God knew what was in front of you when He offered you His coat. He's not surprised by anything that you're facing. God had a plan for Joseph, and He has a plan for you. When Joseph's brothers threw him in that pit, God probably sat in the heavens and laughed: "Look at those boys! They think they're messing up My son. But I gave him My coat. That coat is going to keep him all the days of his life."

When Joseph was sold into slavery, God planned to raise him into a position of authority. By divine coincidence, Potiphar, a very influential man who was captain of Pharaoh's army, bought Joseph. He became Potiphar's chief steward, the keeper of his house. This man's wife could have anything she wanted, anything but Joseph.

> *Now Joseph had been taken down to Egypt. And Potiphar, an officer of Pharaoh, captain of the guard, an Egyptian, bought him from the Ishmaelites who had taken him down there.... Now it came to pass after these things that his master's wife cast longing eyes on Joseph, and she said, "Lie with me." But he refused and said to his master's wife, "Look, my master does not know what is with me in this house, and he has committed all that he has to my hand. There is no one greater in this house than I, nor has he kept back anything from me but you, because you are his wife. How then can I do this great wickedness, and sin against God?"* (Genesis 39:1;7-9 NKJV).

Only one thing can keep you from evil in the day of temptation. If Joseph hadn't been wearing the invisible coat that his heavenly Father had given him, he would have fallen into sin. We live in a world with temptation on every side. Everywhere you look: on every billboard, in every store, and on every television, temptation hits you in the face.

When we first opened our current church building, the neighborhood was so bad that streetwalkers would stand across the street in the morning, trying to stop the guys who were dropping their children off at the church's school. Prostitutes were waiting right across the property line, just 30 seconds out of the anointing. I promise you, if you're not wearing the coat that your Father gave you, you could end up in the bed of a seductress. It's only by the power of God that you will overcome.

Potiphar's wife began trying to seduce Joseph every day, until the final temptation came one day when she caught him alone in the house. Joseph walked in, probably planning to take care of some household business. But Potiphar's wife grabbed him, and propositioned him trying to persuade him that no one would know (see Gen. 39:10-12). But they weren't really alone. Joseph's unseen Friend would know. And His presence prevented Joseph from sinning against God and against his Egyptian master. The house wasn't empty after all, was it?

You see, this invisible coat that Joseph wore—and that we wear today—was not just a coat. It's a person. This coat is God Himself, the Holy Ghost, and He walks with us everywhere we go, empowering and keeping us. Suddenly, the anointing came upon Joseph, urging him to run. That is what you should do in those same moments. Don't just sit there and try to talk or reason your way out of a bad situation. The way to get out is to run. Joseph took off running for his life. Of course, then he faced false accusations. The captain's wife grabbed his coat as he left, screamed, and claimed that Joseph had tried to rape her. Furious with Joseph, her husband threw him into prison (see Gen. 10:12-20).

As the story goes, Joseph stayed in prison until the Pharaoh had a dream that only Joseph could interpret. The interpretation of visions and dreams, a gift of God that Joseph received when his Father's coat came upon him, was what got him out of prison. Through the interpretation of Pharaoh's dreams, Joseph prophesied a seven-year period of abundance in Egypt, followed by an equally long time of famine. As a result, Pharaoh put Joseph in charge of his house and also over all of the land of Egypt. At the age of 30, Joseph became prime minister of Egypt. After being thrown into prison, he was raised up by the supernatural power of God to be the second most powerful man (after Pharaoh) in the entire earth. Finally the famine came for which God, still sitting in the heavens laughing, was waiting. Joseph had stored up so much food for Egypt that he had to stop keeping records.

When the famine came to Canaan, Jacob and his family ran out of food, so he sent his sons to Egypt because he heard there was food there. In Egypt the brothers encountered Joseph, who had become the Prime Minister. Joseph was dressed as an Egyptian, so his brothers didn't recognize him. They bowed down and fell on their faces before him. However, he immediately recognized them and remembered his dream (see Gen. 42:1-9). Eventually Joseph revealed himself to his brothers, and they were afraid, thinking he was going to kill them. Joseph responded, *"And God sent me before you to preserve a posterity for you in the earth, and to save your lives by a great deliverance. So now it was not you who sent me here, but God..."* (Gen. 45:7-8 NKJV).

Through persecution and many troubles, Joseph continued toward the fulfillment of God's purpose and plans for his life. But he was only able to do this because of the invisible coat that his Father gave him, the coat that no man could take from him. He was only able to persevere because of the presence of his invisible friend, the Holy Ghost. God's will is going to be done. You can do it the hard way, or you can do it the easy way. It is the power of the Holy Ghost in your life that will enable you to face the trials, the temptations, and the persecutions.

God blessed Joseph with two children, and the names he gave them are worth studying. *Manasseh*, the name of Joseph's firstborn, means, "God has caused me to forget all my toil and all my father's house" (Gen. 41:51 NKJV). He named his second son *Ephraim*, which means, *"God has caused me to be fruitful in the land of my affliction"* (Gen. 41:52 NKJV). Joseph knew that God had caused him to forget all his troubles. The Lord also helped him understand why he was brought to Egypt in the first place.

He brought him to Egypt so that he could be fruitful and so that he could save his family from starvation.

Sure, at first he must have been angry with his brothers and very disappointed, wondering why God had brought him into all that mess. But the invisible coat that he wore kept burning with the anointing of God. That supernatural coat, that anointing, sustained him through all those years of trouble. Just as He did with Joseph, God will cause you to forget all of the offenses that people have committed against you and all of the things that they have said and done to you. You will forget all of the unfulfilled dreams, the disasters, and the unexpected roadblocks that have hit your life. If you want, you can just sit there wrestling over the difficulties of your life, or you can allow the anointing to help you forget your troubles. The way out of your suffering is to put on the coat and look to Jesus, your unseen Friend.

From the beginning, God had a plan. Jacob returned to Egypt with his entire family, seventy in all. In 400 years, these seventy people became several million. God had caused them to inhabit Goshen, a special land in the midst of Egypt where they were able to prosper (see Exod. 1:1). God prepared them for the day when they would be set free, free to go into the land that He had promised to their great-great-great-grandfather Abraham:

> *And Joseph said to his brethren, "I am dying; but God will surely visit you, and bring you out of this land to the land of which He swore to Abraham, to Isaac, and to Jacob. Then Joseph took an oath from the children of Israel, saying, "God will surely visit you, and you shall carry up my bones from here"* (Genesis 50:24-25 NKJV).

A few years ago, there was a stir in the media with reports that archeologists had found Joseph's bones in Egypt. These researchers discovered a mummy that they thought was Joseph, the great Prime Minister of Egypt. When I read this in the paper, I laughed because I knew that it couldn't really be Joseph's bones. In Genesis 50:25, Joseph took an oath and said, "*...you shall* *surely carry up my bones from here.*" They will never find his remains in Egypt. It would be just as foolish to look for Jesus' bones in a tomb outside of Jerusalem. You can look around and dig in all the graves you want, but you won't find Jesus' bones anywhere on this earth. He was raised up from the dead and seated at the right hand of God. He was given a name above every name. And now He is our unseen Friend.

What an awesome story! Every one of us has faced roadblocks and journeyed on unexpected side trips in life. We've had brothers who mistreated and maligned us, as well as temptations and sin that sought to destroy us. However our story is as simple as Joseph's. It goes all the way back to the very beginning. God is my dad, and I am the favorite son of His love. I will wear the invisible coat that my Father gave me, no matter what the circumstances. That coat is the manifest presence of God. That coat is the Holy Ghost. It is a coat demonstrated by speaking in other tongues, prophesying, healing, miracles, and signs and wonders. It is displayed by casting out devils, by laying hands on the sick, and by not being ashamed of God's power.

Don't be afraid to wear the invisible coat that your Father gave you! It's the only thing that will keep you strong through the trials and temptations of the journey. You might be feeling sorry for yourself. Put on the coat, my friend. Just put it on! I don't care who threw you in the pit, or who lied about you. It doesn't matter what kind of troubles you're going through, just put on the coat. Put on *the garment of praise for the spirit of heaviness.* Put on your dancing shoes. Put on your worshiping outfit and worship before the Lord. Dance in His presence. Come to the world of the supernatural: the world of signs, wonders, and miracles. Take your eyes off of your problems, and put them on the invisible God!

Moses and His Invisible Friend

By faith Moses, when he was born, was hidden three months by his parents, because they saw he was a beautiful child; and they were not afraid of the king's command. By faith Moses, when he became of age, refused to be called the son of Pharaoh's daughter, choosing rather to suffer affliction with the people of God than to enjoy the passing pleasure of sin.... By faith he forsook Egypt, not fearing the wrath of the king; for he endured as seeing Him who is invisible (Hebrews 11:23-25;27 NKJV).

Four hundred years after Joseph was buried in Egypt, another Hebrew, named Moses, was raised as the son of Pharaoh's daughter. This made him grandson and heir to the king of Egypt. Moses was raised in the midst of wealth that we cannot imagine. But when he had come of age, Moses chose what Paul called the *"reproaches of Christ"* (Rom. 15:3) because they were more valuable to him than all the gold and power in the palace.

The reward that Moses received in exchange for his "sacrifice" was the same reward that God gave to Abraham and to Enoch. It was not something measured by natural, tangible wealth. The reward was God Himself. In Genesis 15:1, God told Abraham that He was his reward. In Deuteronomy 10:9, He told the Levites that He was their portion. By faith, Moses forsook Egypt. Have you forsaken Egypt or is Egypt still in your heart? All throughout the Bible, Egypt is a type of the world. The only way to get Egypt out of your heart is to drive it out by getting more of God in your heart. Egypt must be replaced by Zion. The invisible God must replace the visible treasures of this world.

Moses caught a glimpse of a reward more valuable than all the wealth, power, and entertainment that this world has to offer. The angel of the Lord appeared to Moses *"in a flame of fire, out of the midst of a bush"* (Exod. 3:2). As he beheld the bush, it burned with fire, but the bush was not consumed. God said, *"I am who I am."* And He said, *"Thus you shall say to the children of Israel, 'I AM has sent me to you'"* (Exod. 3:14). Moses didn't fear the wrath of the king because he saw a greater king that day in the fiery bush. Once you have trembled in the presence of the almighty, majestic God, the ruler of Heaven and earth, you cannot fear man anymore. Moses didn't care what Pharaoh said or how much power he had. He didn't care how many armies or how much gold he had. He could look Pharaoh in the eye and not be afraid because he had seen the One who we all have to fear. Moses looked at Pharaoh and realized that the king of Egypt was just a coward, hiding behind his gold and his army. How could Moses be afraid? He had been in the fire. He had seen the bush. He had seen the glory. How could he be afraid of a natural man when he had seen this awesome God? Moses had stepped into the presence of the invisible God who inhabits eternity. He saw God for himself. He saw the One who our natural eyes cannot see. Moses glimpsed the King of

Glory with the eyes of his heart, and God was bigger to him than any man or any problem on earth.

As he encountered this awesome God, Moses was on the verge of an incredible journey, a journey of trials and temptations in the wilderness that would last 40 years. It was a journey of danger and responsibility, and the only thing that could sustain him was an encounter with the Holy One of Israel. Moses endured the challenges that he faced *"as seeing Him who is invisible"* (Heb. 11:27). Armed with just a stick, Moses stood on the edge of the Red Sea and looked straight into the face of the most powerful empire that the earth had ever known. This meager instrument was all he had, but it was the tool that the Lord gave him to use against the Egyptians. In the same way, God will give you the tools that you need to deal with the problems in front of you. I have no idea what trials you are facing today, but God knows. What I do know is that the only way for you to endure whatever problem you're facing is to have a heart-encounter with the invisible God. Despite the circumstances, you can endure by seeing with your heart this God who is invisible.

Before his experience with the burning bush, Moses tasted a life like no other. He had dined on the finest foods and partaken of the finest drinks from all over the world. However, Moses had never tasted anything like the One who appeared before him on the back side of the desert. He had lived in the greatest luxury, but it could not compare to the riches of God's presence. Moses had seen the power and authority of Pharaoh, but he had never witnessed such power and authority as he did on the day that he fell on his face before the great I am. From that day forward, Moses walked with his unseen Friend. Wherever he went, I am was his companion. His unseen Friend was there, touching him, speaking to him, empowering him, and equipping him for his journey.

Today, this unseen Friend is still here. The Holy Ghost wants to walk with you, just as He walked with Moses. Have you been in the fire and heard the voice of God? Have you set your eyes on this unseen Friend, this awesome God? Everywhere Moses went from that day forward, he saw this One who is invisible.

From the burning bush, the Lord spoke to Moses and warned him that after all the trials, Pharaoh's heart would be hardened and that he still wouldn't let the people of Israel go free (see Exod. 3:19,20). Frogs, lice, hail, pestilence, and plagues came upon the land. And, as God predicted, Pharaoh did harden his heart. The Lord spoke to Moses, telling him about one last plague. He would kill the first-born of every animal and every family in all the land, including Pharaoh's own son. God instructed Moses to have every Israelite household take a lamb, slaughter it and put its blood on the doorposts of his house. As Moses observed his Jewish brethren, about three million strong, killing the lambs and putting the blood on their homes, and as he did this for his own house, he glimpsed his unseen Friend. This is the Friend who would come to earth thousands of years later as a man. This was the Friend whose blood would be spilled on a cross. His name is Jesus, the Son of God, the Lamb who takes away the sin of the world, the Savior of mankind.

My friends, here we have a picture of how we come into the life of this unseen Friend. Through the precious blood of the Lamb of God, we have access to the incredible presence of God, where our eyes are opened and we begin to see the One who can't be seen. The blood of Jesus is upon our households and upon our lives. I see the handiwork of God in my own life. Washed in the precious blood of Jesus, my conscience is cleansed. He walks with me and talks with me, just like He walked and talked with Moses. I stand in His presence, washed clean in the blood of Jesus. As the Israelites went into their houses that Passover night, they sat down at their tables and began to feast on the lamb that had been slain. The Lord instructed Moses to be sure that the entire lamb was consumed in each household. This lamb would give them strength for their journey, the great exodus from Egypt.

Have you had a taste of the Lamb of God today? Have you tasted His goodness? Have you feasted on God today?

> *Moreover, brethren, I do not want you to be unaware that all our fathers were under the cloud, all passed through the sea, all were baptized into Moses in the cloud and in the sea* (1 Corinthians 10:1-2 NKJV).

As they began to leave Egypt, the Israelites found themselves trapped between the Red Sea and the pursuing Egyptian army. Once again, Pharaoh hardened his heart and prepared to wipe out the children of Israel and take the remainder as slaves. As he stood there, looking at the Red Sea and the advancing army, Moses wasn't afraid. He had been in the presence of the only One who he could ever fear again. He had been in the presence of almighty God. How could he possibly be afraid of man or what man could do to him? In Exodus 14:13, Moses told the Israelites, "*Stand still, and see the salvation of the Lord....*" Moses stretched out his rod and an incredible miracle occurred. The Red Sea opened, and the Israelites walked through on dry ground. When Pharaoh and his army tried to follow them, they all drowned.

As Paul describes the events of that fateful day, he says the Israelites were all baptized in the Red Sea. Like the children of Israel, born-again Christians are baptized as we leave Egypt. As we leave our old lives behind, we experience a death to the life of Egypt, the land of the natural. I no longer live in the land of the flesh and the pleasures of man. I have come out of Egypt. Instead, I have my eyes on the unseen friend that Moses saw on the day that the Red Sea opened. I am following after Him. I too have been baptized. My life has been buried in Christ and I have taken up a new life. I have found my joy now in the presence of God.

Once on the other side of the Red Sea, the Israelites were led through the wilderness by the cloud with the fire in it. Paul says that they were baptized in the water and in the cloud. Have you been baptized in the cloud? Have you been baptized with the Holy Ghost and with the power of God from on high? As you are immersed in that awesome cloud, the Lord will lead you through the challenges of this life. His power and His presence will give you wisdom, direction, and strength. Everywhere that Moses went, he saw the handiwork of the invisible God. He saw Him in the cloud and in the fire. Just like Moses, every day you and I can see the hand of our unseen Friend. Every day of my life, Jesus is there, baptizing me with the Holy Ghost. Every moment of the day, His presence is pouring into me. His glory cloud comes upon me; the fire begins to burn in my heart, and I am filled with His passion again. Have you seen this unseen Friend? Or are you wandering in the wilderness by yourself, depending upon your own strength and your own abilities?

After they got to the other side of the Red Sea, it wasn't long before the Israelites started to complain: "We're all thirsty! Let's kill Moses! Let's stone him! He led us out here to perish in the wilderness!" When they came to the spring at Meribah, they found the water bitter and undrinkable. Then Moses' unseen Friend spoke to him and told him to throw a tree into the waters. Moses obeyed, the waters were purified, and the people began to drink (see Exodus 15:23-27). This tree, a symbol of the cross of Christ, is a picture of the Friend who takes away our sins. On this tree, Jesus bore my curse and removed sin, sickness, and bitterness from my life.

When Moses led the people out, he had no idea what challenges were going to come their way. At one point in the journey, the people fell into sin, and the Bible says that the Lord sent fiery serpents among them (see Num. 21:5-6). Then the Lord told Moses to do something very strange, *"Make a fiery serpent and set it on a pole; and it shall be that everyone who is bitten, when he looks at it, shall live"* (Num. 21:8 NKJV). In this snake, which is a picture of Jesus' death on the cross, Moses glimpsed his unseen Friend who would come and die for all mankind. As Jesus said:

> *And as Moses lifted up the serpent in the wilderness, even so must the Son of Man be lifted up, that whoever*

believes in Him should not perish but have eternal life. For God so loved the world that He gave His only begotten Son, that whoever believes in Him should not perish but have everlasting life (John 3:14-16 NKJV).

Each of us has been bitten by the poison of sin in this world. It comes to us again and again. But as we look to Jesus and the Cross, He delivers us from that snakebite, from the poison that tries to destroy our relationship with God.

Now, as you can imagine, Moses encountered some serious logistical problems while leading three million people in the desert, problems such as getting enough food and water. When the Israelites cried out that they were hungry, Moses' unseen Friend once again answered them in their desperation. Manna covered the ground daily so that they had plenty to eat (see Exod. 16:2-17). Never before had anything like this happened. This physical bread from Heaven was a picture of the true bread that came down from Heaven in the person of Jesus. In John 6:35, Jesus told his followers, *"I am the bread of life: he that cometh to me shall never hunger...."* The manna in the wilderness is a picture of the bread of God's presence, the food that satisfies our hungry souls.

Moses' eyes were on the One you can't see with your natural eyes. He began to see God in everything. Everywhere Moses went, the Lord manifested Himself. He saw God in the sea, in the cloud, in the fire, in the tree that transformed the bitter waters, and in the brazen serpent on the pole. Now, he saw Him in the bread. This holy, invisible presence was with him every day.

The Lord led the Israelites into a place of desolation, so they would see that they couldn't put trust in themselves. Instead they would have to trust Him:

Every commandment which I command you today you must be careful to observe, that you may live and multiply and go in and possess the land of which the Lord swore to your fathers. And you shall remember that the Lord you God led you all the way these forty years in the wilderness, to humble you and test you, to know what was in your heart, whether you would keep His commandments or not. So He humbled you, allowed you to hunger, and fed you with manna which you did not know nor did your fathers know, that He might make you know that man shall not live by bread alone; but man lives by every word that proceeds from the mouth of the Lord (Deuteronomy 8:1-3 NKJV).

God led them into the wilderness, so they couldn't survive on their own, and He humbled them so that they might exalt Him and call out to Him. God fed them with manna, so they wouldn't be proud but would be totally dependent on Him.

Our unseen Friend sustained the Israelites in the form of manna. For us, He speaks to us in the bread of the Word of God. It's interesting to note that God instructed Moses to tell the people to gather only enough manna for one day, no more (see Exod. 16:19-21). In the same way, we can't live off of what we hear preached on Sunday. We have to live off of what we get for ourselves every day. You have to dig around in the Bible every day. You can't depend on your pastor to feed you. Every morning you need to get up and search the Scriptures. We have to hunger for the Word of God, devour the Scriptures, and study to show ourselves approved. We are called to feast on the Word of God every day. This is the message of the manna: we must daily seek our unseen Friend in the Bible.

Have you seen Him in your Bible? The Bible is not a book of rules and regulations, a how-to instruction manual, or a prosperity guide. The Bible is God's revelation of Himself. John 1:14 says that *"the Word was made flesh, and dwelt among us...."* Our unseen Friend lives in this holy book. The natural man doesn't understand it, because the Bible is spiritually discerned (see 1 Cor. 2:14). You need a touch from God. He wants to open your eyes and feed you His manna, just as He daily fed the children of Israel in the wilderness.

The people weren't really happy about the manna every day, even though it was a miracle (see Num 11:4-6). Many people today don't like to get up and read the Bible for themselves every day. However, if you do, you will have a daily miracle just like the Israelites. Your invisible Friend will meet with you. If the Israelites tried to get enough food for two days, the manna would begin to stink and be filled with worms (see Exod. 16:20). You can't live on the revelation that you got yesterday. It doesn't work that way. Our God is a now God. This unseen Friend wants to walk with you every step of every day. He is right here, nearer than you can imagine. He is closer than your skin.

> *"Behold, I will stand before you there on the rock in Horeb; and you shall strike the rock and water will come out of it, that the people may drink." And Moses did so in the sight of the elders of Israel* (Exodus 17:6).

> *...and all drank the same spiritual drink. For they drank of the spiritual Rock that followed them, and that Rock was Christ* (1 Corinthians 10:4).

Just as He provided bread for the children of Israel in the wilderness, Moses' unseen Friend was their source of water as well.

The water that came from the rock is an awesome picture of the only drink that will satisfy a thirsty soul. We need to drink of the Lord's presence every day, drinking in His living waters.

Recently, I was speaking to a pastor friend about chronic dehydration. He said that 80 percent of all Americans are dehydrated. While those figures can be questioned, dehydration is real and can cause severe medical problems. The symptoms that result from natural dehydration, parallel spiritual symptoms that result in spiritual problems that come from a lack of spiritual water. A dry mouth is the first symptom of dehydration. Some Christians have dry mouths. All they talk about are the things of the world, things that don't edify. They never talk about the things of God. Their mouths are full of dryness. Constipation is the second symptom of dehydration. If you don't have enough water in your system, your body can become constipated. This is even true for little babies. They can become dehydrated and experience a lot of pain and discomfort. In the same way, spiritually dehydrated people have difficulty expelling the waste in their lives. They are constipated with the things of this world.

Exhaustion is a third symptom of dehydration. People who don't drink enough of the living water can feel tired all the time. They may think they have no time for the things of God, such as church on Sunday night and Wednesday night. Too tired to go to a home group or to Bible school, they may not even have enough energy to share the gospel or to pray and seek the Lord.

The absence of tears is another symptom of dehydration. In spiritual dehydration, the things of God don't affect you emotionally. Lack of elasticity is the fifth symptom of dehydration. The body starts to age and doesn't repair quickly. Spiritually, this means that a person gets bent out of shape and easily offended. This is a sure sign of someone who is not drinking deeply of the fountain of living water.

One of the most interesting characteristics of dehydration is that people often mistake their thirst for hunger pains, and they think they need to eat. According to the article, if people drank a lot of water before going to sleep at night, they wouldn't wake up feeling hungry. How many people do you know who think they need more teaching when what they really need is a drink from the well of life?

There are some interesting parallels in this illustration and some good spiritual lessons to be learned. I don't want to become spiritually constipated, nor do I want to become tired or emotionally insensitive to the things of God. I don't want to become cranky and carry around offenses everywhere I go. And, believe me, offenses will come. Instead, I want to be thirsty, and I want to drink of the presence of the Lord.

When Moses struck the rock that day in the wilderness, water didn't just dribble forth. The Israelites didn't have to stoop down and lick the rock to get water. No, when water came out of that rock, it gushed forth, providing enough for three million people to drink for 40 years. In the water that flowed from the rock, Moses saw something more than natural water. Moses saw his unseen Friend who sticks closer than a brother, and he must have remembered that first day when he trembled before the awesome presence of the Lord. Moses remembered when he stood before Pharaoh in the power of God, and he remembered the time that the Lord stood beside him on the bank of the Red Sea.

That unseen Friend was with Moses when the Israelites wanted to stone him, and when he came down from the mountain and saw the people's idolatry. He was with Moses when the people began to die because they were being bitten by snakes. The holy, invisible God was with him when armies from all the surrounding nations came against Israel, and He smote the enemies of His people. The Lord was with him every step of the way. In the end, Moses walked up the mountain, looked into the Promised Land, and died. The Bible says in Deuteronomy 34:6 that his secret Friend buried him. His Friend who sticks closer than a brother was with him to the end. This same Friend will take care of you from your first breath to your dying day. He knows where you are, and He is very near to you.

Today is the day that you can begin to depend upon Him who is invisible. This invisible Friend, once a stranger, has become my very best Friend and I know He will never leave me nor forsake me (see Deut. 31:6). He is always there for me. God knows what you are facing today in your family, in your body, in your finances, and in your past. He knows. And He is closer than you think. If you will open your heart to Him, Jesus will give you everything you need on this journey through the wilderness that we call life.

Put the blood on your doorposts, feast on the Lamb, and get strength for the journey. He will strengthen you deep down on the inside. He will make a way where there seems to be no way. He will guide and direct you by His Holy Spirit. He will heal you. He will feed you daily with spiritual food that you gather every day as you search His Word. And He will satisfy your thirsty soul with living water. He's everything you need, this invisible friend, and He longs to come near to you.

CHAPTER 3

The Unseen World of Faith

Now faith is the substance of things hoped for, the evidence of things not seen. For by it the elders obtained a good testimony. By faith, we understand that the worlds were framed by the word of God, so that things which are seen were not made of things which are visible (Hebrews 11:1-3 NKJV).

The unseen world of God, the world of the supernatural, is the world of faith. Faith connects us to God's unseen world. Though forsaken by his brothers, Joseph was not alone. The Holy Ghost, Joseph's invisible coat, was always with him. Moses forsook Egypt, not fearing the wrath of the king, for *"he endured as seeing Him who is invisible"* (Heb. 11:27). Both these men accessed the world of God by faith.

Before he encountered God on the mountain, Moses believed in God. But that encounter changed Moses. No longer did he have merely a mental belief in God, but he had actually experienced God. Everything changed in that moment on the mountain. Moses entered into a new kind of life, a life of dependently living upon God. Of course, before that Moses had believed in the God of Abraham, the God of his forefathers. But until the day that God became a reality in his life, he was not really living upon the invisible God. To be sustained through the next 40 years of incredible trials and incredible blessings, Moses needed not only an encounter with God, but a daily, shared experience with Him.

Living dependently upon the unseen God is the only way to sustain ourselves spiritually in a world that is so crazy, mixed-up, and confused. Filled with temptations, distractions, pitfalls, and side journeys, (both religious and worldly) this world is too much for us to handle alone. Only the faith that comes from a personal experience with the living God gives us the power to meet the challenges we face. He is our source of strength.

John Bunyan authored many great Christian books, including *Pilgrim's Progress*. This small volume has sold more copies that any book other than the Bible. Arrested for preaching the gospel, Bunyan lived in a prison for twelve years. He wrote about "living upon Him who is invisible."[1] This was the theme of his life. It has been said that all of Bunyan's writings had the "smell" of a prison in them. You can sense this same smell when you read the Bible from Ephesians to Revelation. All these books were written from prison too. Not only do they smell of prison, but the fragrant aroma of the Holy Ghost also permeates them.

I don't want to just live in the natural world and smell like the natural world. I want to live in the supernatural world, the world of the Holy Ghost, the world of faith. Living upon the God who is invisible really is the definition of living by faith. I want to smell like the Holy Ghost. I don't want to live by my natural perception, by the way that things look to my eyes, sound to my ears, and feel to my touch. I want to live by faith. I'm not talking about science of the mind or about mind over matter. I am talking about a life of intimacy with God where He becomes the source of all things. I'm talking about a relationship where He becomes my life, carrying me through the things that I face every day.

The writer of Hebrews also highlights the life of Enoch:

> *By faith, Enoch was translated that he should not see death; and was not found, because God had translated him: for before his translation he had this testimony, that he pleased God* (Hebrews 11:5).

Enoch's relationship with God significantly affected the natural world that he lived in. The effect was so great that he was actually ripped out of this world. His spiritual life affected his physical world to the point that he was translated and walked right into Heaven with God. What an awesome thing! Enoch is really a type of the Church that is going to go to Heaven by way of the rapture. A generation like Enoch will arise. They will walk so deeply with the Holy Ghost that they will just walk right into Heaven. Before Enoch's translation, he had a testimony that he pleased God.

Pleasing God requires faith. "*But without faith it is impossible to please Him, for he who comes to God must believe that He is, and that He is a rewarder of those who diligently seek Him*" (Heb. 11:6 NKJV). Here is where we sometimes get confused. God is the reward of faith. Our reward is a relationship with the living God. The eleventh chapter of Hebrews is about great men and women who, by their faith, accessed the world of the invisible God. By faith, Abel offered a better sacrifice and came into the presence of God (see Heb. 11:4). By faith, Abraham walked out of the land of his fathers because he had his eyes on the city whose builder and maker was God (see Heb. 11:8-10).

Faith is not about this world. Faith is about fellowshipping with the other world. Faith is about communicating with the unseen world that is all around us. Our communication with this unseen world, our intimacy and fellowship with God, affects the physical world in which we live. We've had it backward all these years. We have tried to focus our faith on the visible world, asking God to do things for us and to give things to us in the natural world. All we really need to do is put our faith in Him. This is the precious life that God is looking for. He is looking for someone who will diligently seek after Him, who will long for Him and worship Him. When we worship, honor, love, and press in to know God, we receive the greatest reward of all—God Himself.

Most of us have been taught that worship prepares us to receive the Word of God, that the preaching of the Word is the main event of a church service. But in the light of eternity, preaching is not the most important part. We will not need preachers when Jesus comes back. In that day, according to the Bible, we will all be taught of the Lord and the gifts of the Spirit will pass away (see Isa. 54:13; 1 Cor. 13:8-11). Tongues will pass away. Healings will pass away. We will not need words of wisdom or knowledge when Jesus comes. We won't need spiritual gifts and we won't need to teach one another. Teaching, preaching, and the gifts of the Spirit simply prepare us for the big event, which is worship. Once again, we've had it backward. Worship, in reality, is the means by which we live upon the unseen God. As we worship Him, we are filled and satisfied.

In a burst of praise, Paul poured out his heart in a letter to his disciple Timothy: "*Now to the King eternal, immortal, invisible, to God who alone is wise, be honor and glory forever and ever. Amen*" (1 Tim. 1:17). This verse describes how Paul sustained himself when rejected by his friends and his countrymen and when facing the terrible dangers he encountered as he served Christ. These powerful words provide a description of how Paul lived his life, depending upon the invisible God. In the same way, John Bunyan found strength and peace in a life of worship, despite challenging circumstances. Of course, he wanted to be with his family and the church that he had pastored. He wanted his freedom, but he was not willing to sign the statement that his captors wanted him to sign. Bunyan refused to promise that he would never again preach and teach the message of the gospel. If he had done that, he would have been released, but he refused. For those twelve years, John Bunyan lived upon the One who is unseen. God became his source of life. God became his nourishment. God became his all in all.

This kind of teaching is like a foreign language to many people today. Instead, they want to hear about what God will do for them or about what they should do for God. These people are missing the essence of the purpose of our lives on earth. This life really has little to do with the things of the natural world. Life is about this precious treasure that we have in God. Life is about living upon Him. God may not be seen, but He is real. God is invisible, but He is not silent. He is not deaf, and He is not dumb. God's will is that you experience Him every day of your life. He wants to become your life source, not just a "from time to time" experience. Drinking in His manifest presence every day is the will of God for your life.

> *For since the creation of the world His invisible attributes are clearly seen, being understood by the things that are made, even His eternal power and Godhead, so that they are without excuse* (Romans 1:20 NKJV).

On the surface, this statement doesn't even make sense. Paul says that God's invisible attributes are clearly seen, and have been from the beginning of time. Since the day that God created the heavens and the earth, His attributes have not only been seen, but they have also been understood by "the things that are made." This phrase is the Greek word *poeima*, or "poem." *Poeima* means "God's handiwork, His intricate, detailed work." In other words, His invisible attributes are clearly seen by the poetry of His awesome creation.

Paul goes on to say that even God's eternal power is clearly seen in creation. In Romans 1:20, Paul states that a person who refuses to believe in God's existence is "without excuse" because the eternal power of God is clearly seen in creation. Creation reveals the eternal glory of God. His handiwork points us to the invisible God.

When I was a new Christian in Bible school, I read *Foxe's Book of Martyrs*. I didn't want to read it, but it was required by our school. I despised that book because it described a life with which I was unfamiliar. The martyrs had experienced something of God that I had never experienced. I wasn't even sure that I wanted to experience it. I couldn't imagine facing some of the tortures and dangers that these precious men and women of God had endured. I couldn't understand how they were able to face suffering and death with such joy and power. But today it has become much clearer to me. They were living off of the invisible God. They were tasting and enjoying this awesome God, and He sustained them through the worst situations imaginable.

In these days, we cannot live like ostriches with our heads in the sand. These are very dangerous times. The events of September 11, 2001, awakened us. We didn't even realize that such danger existed around us. Serious things are happening in the world right now. It seems like every day you see something in the paper warning about the possibility of nuclear warheads in the wrong hands. Probably other dangers exist that we are unaware. If the world as we know it now was changed in a day, could you live in it? Could you endure the unthinkable? If the whole world entered a time of chaos, could you live upon this unseen God? You could through the outpouring of the Holy Ghost.

God's Holy Spirit is a precious commodity, but He is always accessible and available. We dare not let this precious gift slip through our fingers. We need to embrace God. We need to daily press in to know Him, to worship Him, and to touch the hem of

His garment. In these troubled times, we need to fall in love with Him and drink of His presence every day.

ENDNOTES

1. John Bunyan, *Grace Abounding to the Chief of Sinners* (Hertfordshire, England: Evangelical Press, 1978): 109.

CHAPTER 4

Our Unseen Friend

The people in the Bible experienced things that we can't even imagine. And yet, they were people just like us, with personalities just like ours. They had feelings, passions, and weaknesses, just like we do. The Bible says that Elijah was a man with a nature like ours (see James 5:17-18), and it says that he walked right into heaven. Elijah also prayed and the heavens were shut up for three and a half years. We're not talking about Saint Elijah or Saint Moses. They were regular people, just like you and me. Moses actually killed somebody. He was a murderer who had an encounter with God in a fiery bush. In that encounter, Moses tasted something greater than anything he had experienced before.

Moses grew up in the palace of Egypt, around the greatest wealth existing in the world at that time. Those treasures are exhibited in museums today. In fact, a few years ago the treasures of an Egyptian Pharaoh came to a museum in New Orleans for several months. People lined up by the thousands to take a look at some of the ancient riches of Egypt. Those treasures represented an incredible amount of wealth, and Moses was raised in a palace just like that.

Moses had seen and experienced the best the world of his day had to offer. But one look at the invisible God in the fiery bush changed everything. The value of gold diminished after Moses saw the true treasure in God. He encountered riches that were superior to any wealth this world had to offer him. By faith, he saw the One who is invisible, the One who can't be seen with natural eyes. Moses' spiritual eyes were opened, and God became real to him.

Have you seen Him? Have you glimpsed this One who is invisible? We all have issues. It may not be Pharaoh, but every one of us has outside demands that come beating on our door. Are you approaching your problems in the natural, or have you seen the One who lives in the burning bush? Do you fear Him more than you fear your situations? Have you entered His presence and been touched and edified? Have you tasted His goodness and felt His love?

Remember Paul's prayer in First Timothy 1:17, "*Now to the King eternal, immortal, invisible, to God who alone is wise, be honor and glory forever and ever. Amen.*" That King is walking with you, surrounding you right now. You can access the kind of lives that Joseph, Moses, Enoch, and Elijah had. The Kingdom life is available to every Christian.

The writer of the book of Hebrews describes this Kingdom life of faith as a "new and living way:"

> *Therefore, brethren, having boldness to enter the Holiest by the blood of Jesus, by a new and living way which He consecrated for us through the veil, that is, His flesh, and having a High Priest over the house of God, let us draw near with a true heart in full assurance of faith, having our hearts sprinkled from an evil conscience and our bodies washed with pure water* (Hebrews 10:19-22 NKJV).

He explains how to live a life that is constantly in touch with God. We must live a life of worshiping and breathing in God; we must live for Him and be sustained by Him. Such an awesome life begins through the incredible miracle called Calvary. The blood of Jesus brings us into the presence of God. This is how it begins. You can be saved a hundred years, and you will never get past the beginning. The cross is the centerpiece of our lives. By the precious blood that flowed from our Savior on the Cross, we have access into His presence by faith. We also have access into the life of faith that Joseph, Enoch, Elijah, Moses, and John Bunyan lived.

Our consciences are cleansed and our guilt washed away by the blood of Jesus Christ. His precious blood removes our past sins. I'm not talking about a theology or a philosophy or something you have to believe. I am talking about an experience. The blood of Jesus is not something to believe in intellectually. It is something to embrace. His blood brings us into the holiest place of all. This new and living way—life in His presence—is the way that we touch this unseen friend who is all around us. It's how He reveals Himself to us and how He touches us. What an awesome God! We need access into this supernatural life by faith in the blood of Jesus, and He provides it for us. He is an awesome God, and nothing can wash away our sins but His blood. There is a fountain filled with blood. It flows through Emanuel's veins, cleansing and washing us today.

When tempted by satan during His 40 days of prayer and fasting in the wilderness, Jesus quoted Deuteronomy 8:3, *"Man shall not live by bread alone; but man lives by every word that proceeds from the mouth of the Lord"* (see Matt. 4:4; Luke 4:4). Jesus mentioned this verse to show His utter dependency on God for the ministry that He was about to begin. He humbled Himself, stating that life does not depend upon bread only, but that it exists by the power of the Bread of Life. We have to live and feast on the Word of God every day. We have the power needed to live in His presence, experiencing Him daily, just as Moses did when the manna fell fresh on the ground every day. Don't try to live off of the sermon from last Sunday. Live off of what you ate this morning when you got up and opened your Bible. This is how the Lord wants you to live, surviving by the power of His Word. What I am saying is very simple, but our natural man doesn't want to hear it.

David, another example of a humble man, wrote, *"The Lord is my light and my salvation, whom shall I fear"* (Ps. 27:1a). God anointed him when he was just a teenager. He received a mighty revelation from the Lord, then spent years running for his life, hiding in caves from King Saul. Day to day, David didn't know when he was going to eat or where he would sleep. Pursued for 17 years, he chose to live upon his unseen Friend. Many of his beautiful and inspirational psalms were written while he was running for his life:

> *The Lord is the strength of my life; of whom shall I be afraid? When the wicked came against me to eat up my flesh, my enemies and foes, they stumbled and fell. Though an army should encamp against me, my heart shall not fear; though war may rise against me, in this I will be confident. One thing I have desired of the Lord, that I will seek: That I may dwell in the house of the Lord all the days of my life, to behold the beauty of the Lord, and to inquire in His temple* (Psalm 27:1b-4 NKJV).

David surely was afraid of Saul and of the giant Goliath. He must have had thoughts of fear while being pursued all those years. However, in this psalm, he describes a life experience of touching and living off of the invisible God. David lived a life of worship.

Just like David, you need to have a worship life yourself, a life where you praise the living God in song, both learned and spontaneous. Praise Him with your understanding, and praise Him with your prayer language (see 1 Cor. 14:15). Be filled with the Spirit.

Speak to yourself in psalms, hymns, and spiritual songs (see Eph. 5:19; Col. 3:16). Make a melody with your heart to the Lord (see Ps. 33:2). Access this invisible Friend, this awesome God who is all around you. He is faithful, and He is a friend who sticks closer than a brother (see Prov. 18:24). Come into His presence by the blood of Jesus. Feast daily on the Word of God, and spend time worshiping Him in the Spirit like the Pentecostals used to do. Worship until you feel His presence come down. But it doesn't end there. That is where life with your unseen Friend begins.

When the author of Hebrews wrote to the church in Jerusalem, they had already experienced this life of the Holy Spirit. However, they had begun to return to tradition and formal ritualism. The Book of Hebrews was written to try to bring these people back into the presence of the Spirit and life daily lived in the presence of God. In Hebrews 11, the patriarchs become examples of people who lived this life of faith, this life dependent on the invisible God. The church in Jerusalem was instructed to imitate the faith of these ancient heroes, to walk after God the way that they used to.

> *Therefore we also, since we are surrounded by so great a cloud of witnesses, let us lay aside every weight, and the sin which so easily ensnares us, and let us run with endurance the race that is set before us, looking unto Jesus, the author and finisher of our faith, who for the joy that was set before Him endured the cross, despising the shame, and has sat down at the right hand of the throne of God* (Hebrews 12:1-2 NKJV).

The author was speaking to people who had been in Jesus' meetings, who had seen Him raised from the dead. Some of them were there on the first day of Pentecost, when they were all filled with the Holy Ghost. Encouraging them to look to Jesus, the author and finisher of their faith, the writer of Hebrews urges the members of the Jerusalem church to remember the first day that they were filled with the Holy Ghost, when their supernatural relationship with God began.

In the same way, the Lord has started something supernatural in you, a life in the Spirit. Turn your eyes on Jesus, this unseen God. Don't say that your circumstances are too terrible. Think of John, who was exiled on the island of Patmos for the "crime" of preaching the gospel. Tradition says that the Romans tried to kill him, but that they couldn't. They threw him into boiling oil, but the oil couldn't kill him. So, they put him away on that island because it was the only way to shut him up. How would you feel if you had been taken out of your ministry and away from your family, if people tried to kill you and then threw you onto some island? What if there were no TV crews around or any friends to play games with? What if you were truly alone on that island? What would you have done?

Of course, John wasn't really alone. His unseen Friend was right there, walking with him. On that lonely island, John had an incredible revelation of Jesus. *"I was in the Spirit on the Lord's Day, and I heard behind me a loud voice, as of a trumpet"* (Rev. 1:10). And the wonderful thing is that Jesus had been there all along. Even before John's eyes were opened so that he could actually see Him, Jesus was there. Trying to describe what he saw, John wrote,

> *His head and His hair were white like wool as white as snow, and His eyes like a flame of fire; His feet were like fine brass, as if refined in a furnace, and His voice as the sound of many waters; He had in His right hand seven stars, out of His mouth went a sharp two-edged sword, and His countenance was like the sun shining in its strength. And when I saw Him, I fell at His feet as dead. But He laid His right hand on me, saying to me, "Do not be afraid; I am the First and the Last"* (Revelation. 1:14-17 NKJV).

Imagine seeing what John saw. This unseen Friend can take you through anything. We have tried to focus our faith on things, rather than focusing it on the unseen God and living upon Him who is supernatural. But James 4:8 instructs, *"Draw near to God and He will draw near to you..."* (NKJV). James knew exactly what to do.

What if John had tried to use his faith to get himself delivered from Patmos? What if Daniel had tried to use his faith to get himself released from exile? Or what if Joseph had only sought to be released from prison? Sometimes, even when things look bad, we are exactly where God wants us to be. Press in, get full of God, and watch to see what He will do. When He shows up, you won't care where you are. You won't care if you're on Patmos, in prison, or wherever. You just won't care. Nothing will matter anymore. Keep your eyes on the God who is invisible. Everything changes in His presence. He is our forever and unseen friend.

PART 2

Swallowed Up In God

CHAPTER 1

The Crossroads

[For I always pray to] the God of our Lord Jesus Christ, the Father of glory, that He may grant you a spirit of wisdom and revelation [of insight into mysteries and secrets] in the [deep and intimate] knowledge of Him, by having the eyes of your heart flooded with light, so that you can know and understand the hope to which He has called you, and how rich is His glorious inheritance in the saints (His set-apart ones), and [so that you can know and understand] what is the immeasurable and unlimited and surpassing greatness of His power in and for us who believe, as demonstrated in the working of His mighty strength (Ephesians 1:17-19 AMP).

In this prayer, which begins the Book of Ephesians, Paul calls the Ephesian church to experience something that he has already experienced. "You can hear all sorts of information about God," Paul writes. *"But I want you to taste what I've tasted, to experience what I've experienced, to touch this awesome God who's touched me. I want you to become lost, totally caught up, obliterated, annihilated, and consumed."*

What would it be like if your life was swallowed up in God's life? Paul discovered a whole other world of supernatural experience. As he was traveling on the road to Damascus, his life was swallowed up in God. Life as he knew it was over. God interrupted his life, and Paul couldn't live the way he'd lived before. A line was drawn in the sand.

God became huge in Paul's life. Paul began to see that God was so big, so consuming, that nothing else mattered. God became everything to him, his all in all, his life, his breath, his food, his provision. Paul lost his life that day on the road to Damascus, and he found someone else's life. Paul was crucified with Christ, caught up with God (see Gal. 2:20), and his life was swallowed up. Has your life been swallowed up yet? Has it been so consumed by God that you no longer exist, that you no longer have our own life? Another person has come on the scene in my life. I've been crucified with Christ; nevertheless I live. Yet it's not I who live, but Christ who lives in me. On the road to Damascus, (a road we must all take) we will all eventually run into the God of Jacob, the God of total annihilation, the God who pounds you into the sand and then gives you a new identity.

> *For it is by free grace (God's unmerited favor) that you are saved (delivered from judgment and made partakers of Christ's salvation) through [your] faith. And this [salvation] is not of yourselves [of your own doing, it came not through your own striving], but it is the gift of God; Not because of works [not the fulfillment of the Law's demands], lest any man should boast. [It is not the result of what anyone can possibly do, so no one can pride himself in it or take glory to himself.] (Ephesians 2:8-9 AMP).*

Once you surrender your life to Christ, depending on yourself no longer makes sense. Someone else takes over your life. You become totally dependent on Jesus Christ. Have you gone to the edge of the cliff and told the Lord that you're just going to jump into His arms? It's the leap of faith that will change your life forever. You need to tell Him, "I'm going to trust You. I'm going to be totally dependent on You, and You're going to have to walk with me, carry me, catch me, live in me and live through me. I want my life to be caught up and consumed in yours."

Salvation doesn't come through anything we do. It's a free gift from God. The Creator of the universe comes into our lives and we no longer live. Christ lives and we no longer live. Christ lives in us and we become totally dependent on God. Later in the same letter, Paul wrote:

> *May Christ through your faith [actually] dwell (settle down, abide, make His permanent home) in your hearts! May you be rooted deep in love and founded securely on love. That you may have the power and be strong to apprehend and grasp with all the saints [God's devoted people, the experience of that love] what is the breadth and length and height and depth [of it];[That you may really come] to know [practically, through experience for yourselves] the love of Christ, which far surpasses mere knowledge [without experience], that you may be filled [through all your being] unto all the fullness of God [may have the richest measure of the divine Presence, and become a body wholly filled and flooded with God Himself]* (Ephesians 3:17-19 AMP).

God's love is all consuming. It's a love so huge that it can't be described. It's a love that somehow reaches down and includes each one of us. When we understand this, how can we possibly be caught up with self-love? How can we live consumed with our own needs and desires if we are caught up and consumed with Christ? We need to lose ourselves in the love of God.

What does it mean to be lost in the love of God? When God cares for you, you don't have to care about yourself. Have you ever found somebody who cares more about you than you care about yourself? Jesus put it so clearly: "*Look at the birds of the air, for they neither sow nor reap nor gather into barns; yet your heavenly Father feeds them. Are you not of more value than they*" (Matt. 6:26 NKJV).

If He takes care of the animals, He's going to take care of you. We human beings find it so hard to grasp this concept of the omnipresent love of the Father. Our heavenly Father is constantly caring for us. He never misses a beat. He watches every movement and knows every thought. He never misses anything.

Years ago in Phoenix, Arizona, as I was driving home from work one night, I was worrying about a lot of issues in my life. It was after midnight, and suddenly a sparrow flew into the front of my van and fell to the ground. Immediately, I heard the voice of the Lord say to me, "I knew that bird was going to fall to the ground today. If I know and take care of every sparrow and every thing in this world, don't you know—oh you, of little faith—that I'll take care of you?"

Every movement, every thought, and every gesture that we make is observed by our heavenly Father. We can't miss the love of God. We're surrounded by our Shepherd's love. Our Father has us in His hands, and no one can take us out of His care. Do you think your heavenly Father has forgotten you? Do you think He doesn't know that you exist? You may think He's forgotten your name, or forgotten that you're alive. But He hasn't. He knows exactly what you're facing. and nothing can remove you from His love. He's an awesome God, and He has a great plan for your life.

Before that plan can be fulfilled, however, you have to subject your will to His will. Have you ever thought about unifying your will and God's will? When you allow your will to be consumed in God's will, suddenly His plans will intersect with yours and they'll become one plan. Paul addressed this when he wrote,

I appeal to you therefore, brethren, and beg of you in view of [all] the mercies of God, to make a decisive dedication of your bodies [presenting all your members and faculties] as a living sacrifice, holy (devoted, consecrated) and well pleasing to God, which is your reasonable (rational, intelligent) service and spiritual worship. Do not be conformed to this world (this age), [fashioned after and adapted to its external, superficial customs], but be transformed (changed) by the [entire] renewal of your mind [by its new ideals and its new attitude], so that you may prove [for yourselves] what is the good and acceptable and perfect will of God, even the thing which is good and acceptable and perfect [in His sight for you] (Romans 12:1-2 AMP).

The words, "I surrender my will" can easily get hung up in our mouths. "Lord, I yield my will." My will! One of the first things children learn to say is, "That's mine!" Human nature makes us want to hold on to what we think is ours. But yielding your will to God is such a sweet surrender. Right now, just yield yourself to your heavenly Father. Let your life be consumed, caught up in God's life: "Lord, let my will be lost in Yours. Consume me, Lord. Swallow me up. Let Your will intersect with mine, and let mine get lost in yours. Lord, like Saul on the road to Damascus, let me get lost in Your plans for my life. I want my life to get lost, to the point that I don't even exist anymore."

Paul wrote about one of the main ways that you can loose your self-focus and find your identity in Him:

And all of us, as with unveiled face, [because we] continued to behold [in the Word of God] as in a mirror the glory of the Lord, are constantly being transfigured into His very own image in ever increasing splendor and from one degree of glory to another; [for this comes] from the Lord [Who is] the Spirit (2 Corinthians 3:18 AMP).

When you look into the mirror of God's love, who do you see? What is God's plan for your life? When we consider the truth of God's Word, we look at things that are unseen. We take our eyes off of the visible things of this temporal world, and we put our attention on the invisible truth that is everlasting. As we do this, we begin to be transformed. No longer concerned with self-image, we will find on our identities in Christ. How can we be consumed with our self-image when we've lost our identity in God?

When Paul said, "*I have been crucified with Christ,*" (Gal. 2:20) he was referring to a crossroads in time, to an intersection where one life ceased and another life began. When Paul went to the mirror from that day on, he saw someone different.

The person you used to be doesn't exist anymore. You may be sitting around trying to figure out who you are. "What is my identity?" you may ask. "Who am I?" I'll tell you how the Word of God answers these questions. If you are born again, your identity has been caught up in God. "Who you are" has been lost in who God is. You don't have an identity. Your only identity is Christ. He is your identity! He is your life.

Like Paul, I can say that I have been consumed, swallowed up by God's awesome plan. I feel like Jonah in the whale, swallowed up in God. There has been a divine intersection, a crucifixion of the man I used to be.

In Ephesians 1:18, Paul prays that the Church would have "*the eyes of your heart flooded with light, so that you can know and understand the hope to which He has called you and how rich is His glorious inheritance in the saints (His set-apart ones)*" (AMP). This prayer is particularly significant if we remember that, when Paul was struck down on the road to Damascus, he went blind for three days. When his sight returned, everything was different. Paul was in a different world. From that point on, he saw things differently. After his crossroads experience, Paul's vision changed. God removed the scales from his eyes, and the world looked different. He would never be the same. He had received illumination.

From that day on, Paul could only see Jesus. His prayer in Ephesians 1:17-33 is that we would all walk in the same reality that he had come to know. If what Paul wrote about his experience is true, I guess the question you have to ask yourself is, "Have I been swallowed up?" Has your life been consumed by revival? Have you lost your life so that you can find His? Do you have an intersection in your life where you ceased to exist and where Christ took over? Have you been to that dead-end crossroads?

Let this be the cry of our hearts today: "Lord, open the eyes of our hearts, so we can see Jesus. We want to see Jesus. We want to see the hope of Your calling. We want to see our inheritance in the saints. We want a glimpse of Your glory, Lord. We want to see who You are. We want to see Your greatness. Lord, we don't want to see ourselves. We don't want to see man anymore. We don't want to have a vision of man's plans or man's splendor. We want to see Jesus. We want to see the magnificence of our Savior. We want to see Your greatness and Your majesty. Lord, we want our eyes to be opened. We want to see you, Jesus, no one but You."

David prophesied a day when the people of God would offer themselves willingly to Him:

> *The Lord (God) says to my Lord (the Messiah), Sit at My right hand, until I make Your adversaries Your footstool. The Lord will send forth from Zion the scepter of Your strength; rule, then, in the midst of Your foes. Your people will offer themselves willingly in the day of Your power, in the beauty of holiness and in holy array out of the womb of the morning; to You [will spring forth] Your young men, who are as the dew* (Psalm 110:1-3 AMP).

In this psalm, God the Father promises Jesus the Messiah, "*Your people will offer themselves willingly in the day of Your power.*" This promise describes what our lives are meant to be. It speaks of us making ourselves freewill offerings to our Lord and Savior. It draws a picture of us losing ourselves in God's plan. Are you ready to become a volunteer for God? Will you offer yourself freely in the day of His power? Are you ready to have your life caught up and lost in God? Consumed? Swallowed up?

In the 1950s, a man named Jim Elliot lived in Ecuador as a missionary to the Auca Indians. Facing death as a martyr, Elliot made this famous statement: "He is no fool who gives what he cannot keep, to keep what he should not lose."[1] Are you holding on to what you cannot keep? Why not offer it to God and let yourself be consumed in Him? Only in doing this can you gain what you should not lose.

You see, it's not about your plan. It's about God's plan. It's not about your will; it's about His will. It's not about your purpose; it's about His purpose. It's not about your identity; it's about His identity. It's not about your finances; it's about His finances. It's not about your prayers; it's about His prayers. It's not about your kingdom; it's about His Kingdom. It's all about God! Caught up in Him, He becomes your all in all. He becomes the author and the finisher, the beginning and the end, the Alpha and the Omega. And He can finish what He has started.

The question is, has He started something in you yet? Have you begun the death experience? Has your life been interrupted? Have you had a Damascus Road experience? Do you have a crossroads where you lost your life to gain His? Moses lost his life at the burning bush. Peter made his freewill offering when he left his fishing boat. John's life was swallowed up on Patmos. Paul's life was lost on the road to Damascus. Daniel lost his in the lion's den. Ezekiel, Jeremiah, Abraham— they all shared the same experience. Let today be the day of decision for you. Take the things that you can't hold on to and give them to the only One who can keep you, care for you, and sustain you. Come to the crossroads and begin living a life that is swallowed up in Him.

ENDNOTE

1. Elisabeth Elliot, *Shadow of the Almighty* (United States, Zondervan Publishing House, 1978):

His Love, His Righteousness, His Wisdom

But, on the contrary, as the Scripture says, what eye has not seen and ear has not heard and has not entered into the heart of man, [all that] God has prepared (made and keeps ready) for those who love Him [who hold Him in affectionate reverence, promptly obeying Him and gratefully recognizing the benefits He has bestowed]. Yet to us God has unveiled and revealed them by and through His Spirit, for the [Holy] Spirit searches diligently, exploring and examining everything, even sounding the profound and bottomless things of God [the divine counsels and things hidden and beyond man's scrutiny] (1 Corinthians 2:9-10 AMP).

What kind of experience have you had with God? Is God just a magic genie who you hope will come and make your life better? Or have you allowed Him to completely transform you? I want you to question your experience with the Lord. Like Saul on the road to Damascus, God has planned something much bigger for you than you can even imagine. He wants you to be swallowed up in His life, because His life is so much better than yours. But first you have to let Him take complete control. Let Him substitute His love for yours, His righteousness for yours, and His wisdom for yours. Only when you allow the Lord to swallow you up will you see the miracles that He has in store for you.

> *May Christ through your faith [actually] dwell (settle down, abide, make His permanent home) in your hearts! May you be rooted deep in love and founded securely on love. That you may have the power and be strong to apprehend and grasp with all the saints [God's devoted people, the experience of that love] what is the breadth and length and height and depth [of it]; [That you may really come] to know [practically, through experience for yourselves] the love of Christ, which far surpasses mere knowledge [without experience]; that you may be filled [through all your being] unto all the fullness of God [may have the richest measure of the divine Presence, and become a body wholly filled and flooded with God Himself] (Ephesians 3:17-19 AMP).*

When I came to Christ, my earthly, natural love was swallowed up by the love of God. That's the experience that Paul described to the Ephesians: "My love and the things that I love were swallowed up by the love of God."

Every time I preside over a marriage, I think about how we are so used to depending upon earthly resources. When someone gets married, the natural marriage—without the supernatural element—is dependent on human love. It is doomed to failure, regardless of whether it culminates in divorce or in two miserable people living in the same house.

Human love is limited. It will always let you down. Human love is selfish, based on, "If you give me what I want, I'll give you what you want." That's human love. That's the flesh. But Paul told the Ephesians about another kind of love. This love came down and swept him away. It reached down to the depths of his depravity, his misery, and his sinful condition, and it lifted him up.

This is one of Paul's favorite messages. In fact, it is the theme of his life: the Lord loved me, embraced me, and included me, and His love has just swelled me up. Like Paul, I want you to know this overwhelming love of God. This love is not learned. It can only be experienced. It has to be tasted.

This love is the only way to truly know God, to be pleasing to Him. Paul wrote about this to the Philippians:

> *Circumcised the eighth day, of the stock of Israel, of the tribe of Benjamin, an Hebrew of the Hebrews; as touching the law, a Pharisee; concerning zeal, persecuting the church; touching the righteousness which is in the law, blameless. But what things were gain to me, those I counted loss for Christ. Yea doubtless, and I count all things but loss for the excellency of the knowledge of Christ Jesus my Lord; for whom I have suffered the loss of all things, and do count them but dung, that I may win Christ. And be found in him, not having mine own righteousness, which is of the law, but that which is through the faith of Christ, the righteousness which is of God by faith* (Philippians 3:5-9).

In this passage, Paul says, "I was a strict follower of the scriptures. I fasted regularly, prayed regularly, tithed regularly. I did my religious duties. I performed all the vows of a Nazarite, and I went through all the rituals of a Pharisee." Paul followed the law to the dot. He knew the Torah, and he followed every letter of it. But a day came when Paul realized that obeying the law and trying to be justified by his own actions and abilities was hopeless. God swallowed him up, and he discovered that life in God is what it's really all about. "I used to know a form of righteousness, but I was deceived," Paul says to the Philippians. "I thought

I was righteous because of all my actions—because I prayed, tithed, and obeyed the law. Because I did all these wonderful things, I thought they made me pleasing before God. Now I realize how wrong I was."

None of those things can ever be good enough to please God, because sin is a part of our DNA. It was part of Paul's life. It was in him, and he didn't know it until the day when he came face to face with the righteous One. As he stood naked before the Lord, his own righteousness—based on the law, based on his own actions, based on his own strength, and based on his own abilities—was swallowed up in God's. Paul was swallowed up in God, and God's righteousness came upon him. "I saw Him, and my sins were exposed," Paul tells the Philippians. "He took from me those filthy garments that I was so proud of, those garments of my accomplishments, and he put upon me the garment of righteousness that only comes through faith. It only comes from God." So Paul's righteousness was consumed, as he was lost in God.

> But rather what we are setting forth is a wisdom of God once hidden [from the human understanding] and now revealed to us by God—[that wisdom] which God devised and decreed before the ages for our glorification [to lift us into the glory of His presence]....But the natural, nonspiritual man does not accept or welcome or admit into his heart the gifts and teaching and revelations of the Spirit of God, for they are folly (meaningless nonsense) to him; and he is incapable of knowing them (progressively recognizing, understanding and becoming better acquainted with them) because they are spiritually discerned and estimated and appreciated (1 Corinthians 2:7,14 AMP).

The wisdom of man is actually what keeps us from possessing the wisdom of God. Confidence in our own wisdom, our own strength, and our own goodness blocks us from receiving what the Lord wants to give to us. Some people are proud of their physical achievements, some people are proud of their religious achievements, and some people are proud of their intellectual achievements. All of these things are not evil in themselves, but confidence in them will keep you from God.

There's a wisdom that the natural man cannot grasp—God-given wisdom. God is the only One who can give us true wisdom. On the road to Damascus that day, God came down and revealed Himself to Paul. God did it. The Lord opened Paul's eyes, so he could understand the spiritual wisdom that is found only when you are swallowed up in God.

When you encounter Jesus, you touch wisdom; you touch righteousness, and you touch love. He is all in all. He's everything we need. When Paul was swallowed up in God on the road to Damascus, he realized, "This is righteousness. I can no longer trust in my own righteousness. This is love. I cannot trust in my own natural, human love. This is wisdom. I can no longer be proud of my own studies and my own research. This is glory. I can no longer glory in my own accomplishments." You cannot serve God in your natural strength. You can't. It has to be supernatural. But once you allow Him to swallow up your love, righteousness, and wisdom in His, then you will see Him begin to move in your life.

What would it look like if God visited you today? How would you be changed if He swallowed you up? When God visited Sarah, she began to laugh. But the lasting result of that visitation was the miraculous birth of her son Isaac. She had longed for a son since her youth, and finally at the age of 90 she received her miracle.

Maybe there's something in your life that God promised you a long time ago, and now you've given up. Sometimes the Lord waits until you give up. He waits until you've tried everything. He'll sit there and say, "Are you finished yet?" Are you finished? Can you say, "I've fasted, I've prayed in tongues, I've done everything"? His answer to you is: "*Be still and know that I am God.*

Cease striving and know that I am God" (see Ps. 46:10). How awesome He is!

One of the ways that God revealed Himself through Jesus—and later through the early church—was by the working of miracles. These miracles glorified God. When you think about the ministry of Jesus, you can't help but think about His healing miracles. The river of healing is unlimited. It never stops. No condition is too hopeless for God. In His mind, no physical condition is beyond repair. When you think of the miracles of Jesus, you remember people who were maimed, blind, paralyzed, and diseased. Each was restored and made whole.

Nothing is too hard for God. But first, our strength has to be swallowed up in His. As we surrender our human love, our own righteousness, and our worldly wisdom, the Lord takes hold of us and swallows up our weaknesses. Maybe your marriage needs to be swallowed up. Maybe your finances need to be swallowed up in the presence of God. Maybe your physical body is sick. Isaiah prophesied, *"He will swallow up death in victory; and the Lord God will wipe away tears from off all faces; and the rebuke of his people shall he take away from off all the earth: for the Lord hath spoken it"* (Isa. 25:8).

Has your life, your strength, been swallowed up yet? That's the place where miracles happen. It does God no good at all to heal someone who is still doing his own thing. My dad died of lung cancer, but he would never completely surrender his will to God. He smoked cigarettes until the end of his life. He prayed and submitted his life to the Lord at the very end, but prior to that he was totally determined that he was going to keep doing what he wanted to do.

What would it look like if God visited you with a miracle today, if you got what you've been waiting for? I'm not talking about the manifestation that would happen right now. I want to know how your life would be changed a month from now. I like to think of blind Bartimaeus, lying there in his beggar's garments.

Those garments were his only means of living, but when Jesus of Nazareth came by, Bartimaeus threw them away and his eyes were opened. My favorite part of this story is the way it ends. The Bible says that Bartimaeus followed Jesus down the road (see Mark 10:46-52). That's how it ends. He didn't just get healed and then go back to his old life. He got healed, and he lost his life. His old life was swallowed up in God's life, and he followed Jesus down the road.

If you were healed, what would you do with your healing? If the Lord blessed you financially in a major way, what would you do with your financial blessing? If He came down and visited you, would you follow Him down the road? Are you following Him down the road now? Or are you just saying, "Lord, I need you. Help me, Lord. Won't you help me, God? I'm in trouble"? When you allow yourself to be transformed, to be swallowed up in God, He will substitute His love, His wisdom, and His righteousness for yours. He will consume your weaknesses and your problems in His awesome, miraculous healing power.

CHAPTER 3

Past, Present, and Future

The story of Jonah is really the same story as that of the apostle Paul. They both got swallowed up by God. Each of these awesome men of God surrendered his will to God and saw how the Lord transforms the past, present, and future in our lives. God spoke to Jonah and said, "I want you to go to Nineveh" (see Jon. 1:1-2). Nineveh, the capital of Assyria, was a pagan city, and God said, "I want you to go to this place of idolatry and abomination, and I want you to prophesy. Tell the people that if they don't repent, their city is going to be destroyed."

This was a very radical thing for God to tell Jonah to do. Assyria was a pagan nation and the Jews would have nothing to do with Gentiles. Well, Jonah refused to do it. He said, "Lord, I'm not going to go there." He ran from God's plan for his life. *"Jonah rose up to flee unto Tarshish from the presence of the Lord..."* (Jon. 1:3).

Have you ever run from the presence of the Lord? Jonah found a ship going to Tarshish. He paid the fare and tried to run from the will of God. But Jonah found that you can't hide from the presence of the Lord. He is everywhere.

> *But the Lord sent out a great wind into the sea, and there was a mighty tempest on the sea so that the ship was like to be broken....So they [the sailors] took up Jonah, and cast him forth into the sea: and the sea ceased from her raging....Now the Lord had prepared a great fish to swallow up Jonah. And Jonah was in the belly of the fish three days and three nights (Jonah 1:4,15,17).*

This fish was a place of appointment for Jonah, where he had to go to meet God. He was being swallowed up by God. When God has a plan for your life, you don't have many choices. You might think you do, but that fish is waiting for you, I promise. God has appointed a fish for each one of us.

From inside the fish, Jonah prayed to the Lord, and the Lord heard his cry and caused the fish to vomit him onto dry land (see Jon. 2:1-10). Of course, when he submitted himself to God and was vomited out onto the land, Jonah went to Nineveh and prophesied as the Lord had commanded. The whole city called a fast and repented, and the judgment was stayed (see Jon. 3:1-10). Jonah did not want to go to Nineveh, but God said, "You're going. One way or another, you're going. You can do this the easy way or the hard way." Jonah's story could be your story too. Unfortunately, most of us take the hard way, just like Jonah.

Paul's story is similar to Jonah's. Like Jonah, Paul had a calling on his life to go to the Gentiles. And like Jonah, Paul fought God. On the road to Damascus, he thought he was serving God. But breathing out threats, Paul was actually working to disrupt the plan of God. He was rooting out pockets of Christians in an attempt to stop a "cult" that threatened his faith. And while he was on his way to Damascus to persecute more Christians, Paul had a visitation from God. A light came down from Heaven and he was struck blind, overwhelmed by the presence of the Lord (see Acts 22:6-11). Trembling and astonished, Paul asked, "Who are you,

Lord?" And the Lord replied, "I'm Jesus, Why are you kicking against the pricks?" Sent by God to Damascus, Paul discovered the call upon his life:

The God of our fathers has chosen you to know his will and to see the Righteous One and to hear words from his mouth. You will be his witness to all men of what you have seen and heard (Acts 22:14-15 NIV).

From this point on, Paul's life was no longer his own. He had experienced a violent interruption. That's what salvation is. It's so much more than being able to say, "OK, now my sins are forgiven, and I'm going to heaven." Salvation is a violent intervention in our lives. With Jonah and with Paul, God came down and swallowed up their lives. On the road to Damascus, Paul had a plan to do something, and his will was just swallowed up by God's will. It was gone! Jonah's plan to run from the presence of God vanished when he met the fish. God intervened and took the place of their wills for their lives.

This is a picture of what happens to us. God has a plan for your life, and He's not really interested in your plan. When you touch the real thing, when you touch God and God touches you, it's not a matter of thinking, "OK, now God's going to come into my life and cause everything that I want for my life to happen. He's going to come and fix my life for me." That's not what salvation is. That's not what Christianity is about. Christianity is a death experience. At salvation, your life is finished. Finished. It's over. A crucifixion takes place and a burial. Baptism is a burial service. When people die, we give them decent funerals. That's what water baptism is: a burial service that says, "My life is finished. My will is over. Someone else has taken over my life."

When God swallows you up, He leaves a mark on your life. Can you imagine the effects of the fish's stomach acid on Jonah's body? He must have been bleached—his hair, his skin. In the same way, God wants people to notice that something's happened to you. "Why do you look like that? What's happened to you?"

"Well, I was in a belly of a fish that swallowed me." As he was on his way to Damascus, Paul's life was swallowed up by God. He was engulfed by God's presence. That's God's plan: for His life to devour your life, for His glorious presence to consume your past, present and future. Now, this is not a very popular message, because when most people discover the love that God has for them, they misread and misunderstand it. The discovery of God's incredible love makes people think that they are the center of His universe. They imagine that it's all about them and what God can do for them. But at some point in your life you must realize, "It's not about me at all. It's all about Him."

My past needed to be swallowed up, to be eaten by a big fish. The Holy Ghost whale comes and eats us. He'll devour all of your sinful past, all the stuff that you wish you'd never gotten into, the stuff that messed up your life. When you are swallowed up by God, His presence consumes all the stuff that caused you to mess up your marriage, your family, and your relationship with your parents. God wants to swallow everything that has devastated you, everything that has disrupted and destroyed your life. When this awesome God comes to us and we surrender our lives to Him, our pasts are consumed. Our sins are cast into the depths of the sea, removed as far as the east is from the west (see Ps. 103:12). Not only are your sins forgotten, but so are your offenses, hurts, and wounds from other people.

When we lived in Phoenix, Arizona, we couldn't afford to buy a dog, so we went to the animal shelter and got one. This dog looked beautiful, but he was really messed up. He had some big time baggage. I have no idea what his past was like, but often, while we were just sitting around, this dog would go into a fit. He would run wildly, spinning in circles and frothing at the mouth; then he would fall to the ground. After a few minutes of this, he would sit down and act like a normal dog again. Of course, since we had little babies in our house, we had to return the dog after a few of these episodes. There's no telling what that dog had experienced that would cause him to have those fits.

Maybe some of you are a little like this dog. You look OK on the outside, like everyone else, but occasionally you just take off and have a fit. Everyone thinks you're normal, but it's just a big show. Inside you just hope you can hold it together.

The Bible says that the blood of Jesus is able to cleanse our consciences, our memories of our past lives and the horrible things that have been done to us. I don't know what kind of abuse you experienced or what kind of baggage you're carrying around. I don't know why you twitch the way you twitch. But I do know that when you get swallowed up by God, it will be as if that old life never happened. Sometimes people want to dig up the past and start talking about the horrible things that happened to them. They start describing all these events in great detail. Before long, everybody is crying. I was in one service where they had an altar call for people who had been abused in their mothers' wombs. People came up and were brought through a process of deliverance. They simulated being birthed and falling into a blanket, and as they did this, they were screaming out all kinds of things. This was supposed to be a Holy Ghost service, but what no one seemed to realize was that all that stuff had already been swallowed up.

Nothing that happened to me before that Holy Ghost fish ate me applies to my life anymore. I've been crucified with Christ, and that old person doesn't exist anymore (see Gal. 2:20). Whatever happened to him doesn't matter anymore. My conscience has been cleansed, cleansed of the hurtful things that I did to other people and cleansed of the hurtful things that other people did to me. My past is the past, and it's over. Swallowed up in God, I don't have to dig up those old skeletons and cry over them again. They're gone. Finished. Swallowed up in God.

Just like your past, your future can also be swallowed up in God. Jonah's was. He thought his future was somewhere else—on that boat to Tarshish. But God had another plan, and Jonah was swallowed up and spit back to Nineveh. Paul's future changed completely after his encounter with Jesus on the road to Damascus. Ananias prophesied that Paul had been chosen to know the will of the Lord, to hear His words and to be a witness to all men of what he'd seen (see Acts 22:14-15). On the road to Damascus, Paul surely had some plans for his life. He had plans to go to other cities, continuing his persecution of the Christians. But his future plans were devoured by God. When God came down and touched Paul, not only were his plans eradicated, but his future was too. Has your future been swallowed up in God yet?

When our lives are consumed in God, a beautiful thing begins to happen. We yield our plans to God and say, "Lord, I'm not concerned about the plans that I have for my life anymore. I'll just leave everything in Your hands." In this place, God begins to speak to us. Line upon line, precept upon precept, He begins to speak, giving us glimpses of His plans for our lives. God has a plan for your life. Are you willing to let your plan be swallowed up? I am describing a life of incredible victory and joy. Jesus said that if you seek to save your life, you'll lose it (see Luke 9:24). If you try to pursue your plan, you'll miss out on His. I'm sick of the message that Christianity is all about us just bringing all our wants and needs to God. I am tired of people looking at God as a free ticket to do whatever they want. No, No, No! I'm supposed to do whatever He wants. When I am swallowed up in God, He changes my will. Doing His will becomes the joy of my life.

Until you surrender to that big fish, you will never be happy. You'll never be satisfied. You'll wander as a restless soul from church to church. Caught between the world and the realm of the Holy Ghost, you'll know that the world is not the way to go, but you won't yet yield to the plan of God for your life. You'll be a miserable person, wandering around between the two worlds. Jonah knew that he couldn't just be a worldly guy. But at the same time, he didn't want to yield to God's plan, so he ended up in the belly of a whale.

The sweetest place is when you say, "I surrender, Lord. I surrender." This is a place of peace, where you just have a feeling that everything is going to work out OK.

And the strangest part is that the thing that you were striving so hard to get will fall into your lap when you give it up to God, when you say, "God, I'm just going to serve You. I'm not going to worry about my future plans anymore." Maybe you're so bound up looking for a spouse that you can't see straight. You've made a list of requirements, including eye color and hair color. You're believing, you're confessing, and you're sowing. You're trying to make it happen. Just give it up. You'll find that person waiting for you in the fish's belly. If that person you're pursuing is not in the fish's belly, then you don't want him or her! Whatever plans you've made for your life, let them be swallowed up in God's future for you. Whatever it is, just give it up.

Just as your future and your past can be consumed in God, so can your present. Jesus says to you,

> *Come to me, all you who are weary and burdened, and I will give you rest. Take my yoke upon you and learn from me, for I am gentle and humble in heart, and you will find rest for your souls. For my yoke is easy and my burden is light* (Matthew 11:28-30 NIV).

No matter what your circumstances are, they can be swallowed up in God. I don't care what your problems are, how big or small. Regardless of whether you have cancer in your body, a divorce pending, a bankruptcy looming, a child in rebellion, or any other kind of disaster hanging over your head, your present circumstances can be swallowed up by God. As a matter of fact, Jonah had some circumstances that he was dealing with in his life. Jonah was facing a life-threatening storm.

Problems in our lives can cause us to do one of two things: they can cause us to be bitter and run away, or they can cause us to come to God. We can blame other people for our problems, or we can press in to God. You can blame your parents, your friends, or your spouse, but eventually you'll probably realize that you got into your mess all by yourself, without anyone else's help.

The Lord swallows up your present situation, your "right now." Your sickness is swallowed up in His healing. Your poverty is swallowed up in His provision. Your depression is swallowed up in His joy. Just cast your cares upon the Lord (see 1 Pet. 5:7). Cast your burden upon Him. Take His presence upon you, and let it consume you.

Jesus wants to heal your body. Those wounds on His body purchased you, your whole being—spirit, soul, and body. Do you believe it? Your health was purchased by the stripes of Jesus Christ. He can swallow you up in His presence and heal your body. Not only does He provide healing in the belly of the whale, He also releases provision. He gives forgiveness. He brings deliverance. And He fills you with joy. He offers freedom from the past and hope for the future. Run into Him. Press into Him. Let your life be swallowed up in God.

PART 3

The Promise of the Father

CHAPTER 1

The Inheritance

One summer, my family and I traveled to the north-western United States, where I ministered in a couple of churches, and we took a few days of vacation. I am in love with God's creation in southeast Louisiana, and I have talked a lot about its swamps, alligators, and other animals, but we saw a whole different part of God's handiwork on this trip.

We visited Mount St. Helens, the volcano that erupted several years ago. Even to this day, for miles and miles around, all you see is ash, burned-down, empty forest land, and miles of nothing. Man thinks he is so wonderful and so powerful, but he is nothing compared to the tremendous power of God's creation.

We also took a boat ride just off the coast of Washington and about 30 killer whales, 35 to 40 feet long, came near to our boat. Along the coast's edge, people in kayaks were paddling among this pod of killer whales. No amount of money could have convinced me to get into one of those kayaks. The whales would jump totally out of the water, and we could see their faces. They are just one of the millions of God's creatures. Our God is an awesome God. He is past comprehension.

When you begin to become aware of God, you see Him everywhere. God's love constantly cries out all around us. When He touches you, and He becomes a reality in your heart and in your daily life, you start seeing Him everywhere you go. David knew this. In Psalm 19:1, he cried out, *"The heavens declare the glory of God...."* Moment by moment, creation utters forth God's glory. Man's problem is that he is only in touch with the natural and not with the supernatural. But once the connection between natural and supernatural takes place and you start to live in the awareness of the realm of God, everything takes on a different look. Everything becomes brand new to you. God is so awesome, so overwhelming, so far beyond our natural comprehension. When we get little glimpses of how great He is, we end up on our faces before Him. The most amazing thing is that He has chosen us to be His children. He is our Father, not some ogre who lives millions of miles away. Our Father has chosen us to be His sons and His daughters. As the children of God, we become His heirs.

In Galatians 4, Paul demonstrates the difference between the law and grace by explaining how heirship works:

> *As long as the heir is a minor, he has no advantage over the slave. Though legally he owns the entire inheritance, he is subject to tutors and administrators until whatever date the father has set for emancipation. That is the way it is with us: When we were minors, we were just like slaves ordered around by simple instructions (the tutors and administrators of this world), with no say in the conduct of our own lives. But when the time arrived that was set by God the Father, God sent His Son, born among us of a woman, born under the conditions of the law so that He might redeem those of us who have been kidnapped by the law. Thus we have been set free to experience our rightful heritage. You can tell for sure that*

you are now fully adopted as His own children because God sent the Spirit of His Son into our lives crying out, "Papa! Father!" Doesn't that privilege of intimate conversation with God make it plain that you are not a slave, but a child? And if you are a child, you're also an heir, with complete access to the inheritance (Galatians 4:1-7 TM).

I have always struggled with the verbiage in this passage and also with Romans 8:15 where it says that He sent the "Spirit of adoption" into our hearts. The concept of being an adopted child has always bothered me because of one issue that I didn't understand about it.

Many adopted children live in wonderful homes with great parents who take good care of them, but something deep down inside of them wants to know about their biological parents. They want to know where they came from. When I was growing up, one of my best friends was adopted. His parents never told him that he was adopted, but he knew that he was. His parents were fair skinned, Anglo-Saxon people of average height, and my friend had dark skin and dark hair and was about one and a half feet taller than his dad. He had obviously looked at his mom and dad and realized that they weren't his biological parents. It didn't take a genius to figure it out. Nevertheless, they didn't tell him. Even though he knew his parents loved him, my friend always struggled with who he was. He struggled all his life with questions like, "Who am I?" "Where did I come from?" and "What is my origin?"

When I would look at God's adoption of us, I thought it was wonderful that He adopted us and gave us a break. But then I realized that a difference exists between adoption in the natural world and adoption in the spiritual world. The Bible says that God sent the "Spirit of adoption" into our hearts (see Rom. 8:15). As an adopted child in the natural world, you cannot take on the biological nature of your adoptive parents. You cannot take on their chemistry. They can love you. They can provide for you. They can be your father and your mother in every sense of the word, but biologically you didn't come from them. The Bible says that when we became children of God, He sent His Seed, His Word, and His Spirit into our hearts, not symbolically but in reality (see 1 Peter 1:23; II Peter 1:3,4). He planted the essence of God inside of you when you accepted Him as your Savior. He placed the nature of the Holy One within you. A royal seed was planted inside your heart. It's different from what the world has. We are connected with our Heavenly Father by more than just a legal contract in which He has agreed to provide us with food, lodging, work, and eternal life.

I don't want an arrangement like that, where I never get to see the Father, where I just have all my needs cared for. My greatest need isn't my physical provision. My greatest need is to be loved. My greatest need is a relationship. Our Father does much more for us than just meet our physical needs. Out of a thankful heart we cry, "Lord, we love all the gifts that You give us. Lord, we appreciate all that You do for us. Thank You, Lord, for the great job. Thank You, Lord, for the car. Thank You, Lord, for the clothes You have given me. Thank You, Lord, for everything that You have provided. But, Lord, more than anything, I thank You that You have given me Yourself so that I can know You, so that I can walk with You."

The Bible says that we can tell for sure that we are fully adopted as His children because God sent the Spirit of His Son into our lives, crying out, "Papa, Abba, Father, Daddy, I love You" (see Gal. 4:6). The privilege of intimate conversation with God proves that you are not a slave, but a child. In Galatians 4:7, Paul goes on to say that if you are a child of God, then you are an heir with complete access to your inheritance. The inheritance that God gives you when you become His child is not something that you receive only when you die. You have access to His inheritance today. You can step right into it. What a shame for someone to have everything they need and to never get the benefit of using it. What a shame to have all the wealth you need provided for you and to never know how to access it. What a shame it would be if someone died and left you millions of dollars but the money never reached you because you never knew about it. Even though you had millions of dollars sitting in the bank, you would never benefit from it. You could live in a shack on the bad side of town because you didn't know.

Most Christians don't know about our spiritual inheritance as children of God. They think that our inheritance is somewhere in the future. They think it is something they get when they die. They think they just get a mansion in glory someday. But the inheritance is ours now. We are children of God. Our inheritance is not going to come to us in the future. It has already happened. Our Heavenly Father has already given His Son. His Son has already been raised from the dead. He has already sent the Holy Ghost, the Spirit of adoption, the Spirit that makes us His children. He has sent the Spirit into our hearts and we cry out, "Father, I love You." He says, "I love you, son. I love you, daughter. You are my special child. There is no one quite like you. I like the way you smile."

Your Father likes the way you smile. He likes the way you look at Him. He likes the way you respond when His presence touches you. He loves it. You are His child. He can't stand to be away from you. He loves the way that you act. He loves the way that you talk. He knows that He made you that way. Hallelujah! You are His special child. You are His chosen child.

Our Father sent His Holy Ghost presence into our hearts. That is what the current outpouring and revival is all about. It is nothing more than an experience with God, with His presence. All that you see taking place as a result of this revival is a response to the presence of God and to His glory. People are being touched with the real presence of God. Some are so excited that they can't keep their feet still. Overwhelmed with joy, they have to take off running, dancing, or leaping. Or they can't stand up anymore. They are so overwhelmed by God's love that they have to lie down on the floor and just enjoy His presence. They are overwhelmed by the reality of His love. God is real. His presence is real. Your Heavenly Father wants you to experience the intimacy of His presence in your life. This is part of your inheritance as His child.

The Bible has many examples of the principle of inheritance. The Father gives His blessing to us like Jacob gave his blessing to his son Joseph. Jacob gave Joseph the coat of many colors because he loved him. It was the coat of his favor, the coat of anointing, the mantle that he placed upon Joseph. In Jesus' parable, the prodigal son came back because he didn't like being away from his father's love. When he first left home, the prodigal son thought that the important parts of his inheritance were the money, the wealth, and all the good gifts. But after he went away, he realized that what he missed most of all wasn't his bed and the warm meals on the table. What he missed most of all was his father's love (see Luke 15:11-32). When you are not right with God, you miss His love. You try to satisfy your longing for love in the natural world. You try to satisfy that need in illicit relationships, looking for love with a man or a woman, or you seek satisfaction in a new job, a new car, or a new house. But something new will never satisfy your longing, because what you need deep down inside is not the love of a man or a woman or the possession of some tangible thing. What you need is the gift of God's presence. It is His love, the Father's love.

When we accept Jesus, we step into the inheritance that God has for us. The greatest part of that inheritance is the new nature He puts inside us. He has put into us a nature that is not contaminated by the desire for the things of this world. Instead, we have the Father's seed inside of us. As we nurture this relationship with Him, God changes us from glory to glory to glory; and we become more like Him (see 2 Cor. 3:18). We begin to have the Father's heartbeat inside of us. We start to resemble the

Heavenly Father. In John 14:9, Jesus said, *"He who has seen Me, has seen the Father..."* (NKJV). The Father is real. His presence is real. His love is real. When we step into our inheritance, we realize that a change is taking place inside of us. We start to discover our new nature. Then we begin to realize that the tangible comfort of God's presence can be with us all the time. This is part of our inheritance.

I don't know where we Christians learned it, but for years we did not take our rightful inheritance. Over the years I have taught a lot about the gifts that God has for us, and I believe that He does want to bless us with natural things. I believe that God wants to heal our bodies and that He wants to provide for our financial needs. But our true inheritance is much more than all of this. His real, tangible presence is one of the essential elements of our heritage. What a shame it would be if you didn't experience God's presence every day of your life and if you didn't realize that you can live by walking in the Spirit. You would miss out on your heritage as a child of God. It would be like receiving all sorts of gifts and not knowing what they were or being able to enjoy them.

Many people don't experience God's presence, either because they don't know it's available or because they think it's not really worth having. But I am telling you, it is the best gift! Some people know that the presence of the Lord is real, but they are afraid to get too close because of what it will cost them. Their fear is rooted in fouled-up value systems. They are afraid that they might have to give up their video poker games, their weekly lottery tickets, and their after-dinner drinks. Some people are afraid to get too close to the fire. These people are looking at everything they think they will lose, but they have no idea what they will gain.

I remember when I was 21 years old and the Lord was dealing with me just weeks before I got saved. I took out this scraggly bag of marijuana that was full of twigs and seeds. I thought, "Man, I'm going to have to give this up." The problem was that I did not know what I was about to gain. When God touched me and touched my life, that bag of marijuana became the most ridiculous thing to me.

Who can compare the presence of God, the glory of God, to a scraggly old bag of dope? What can compare? "Lord, I really enjoy this apple wine." Who could have known? I was hanging on to natural wine, not even realizing that I could drink a spiritual wine that was far superior to the natural stuff. Once you have tasted the true wine, you will never settle for that cheap stuff again. We look at the things of the natural world, unaware of the reality of the presence of God. We do not understand the Father's inheritance. The prodigal son had the same problem. He did not see the real value of his inheritance. He thought that if he could eat pig food he would really be living in style. But he was missing out on the real pleasure that he was born to enjoy. He was missing out on his father's love.

We were created for one purpose—to be loved by our Heavenly Father. The whole Bible from Genesis 1 through Revelation 22 is the story of our Father and His family. It is the story of a Father who longed to have children He could hold in His lap and pour all of His blessings upon. Your Father wants to give you His love. He wants you to taste His love. When you taste this royal heritage, you put on the King's garment. When you wear the Lord's mantle and have His ring on your finger, you are walking in the inheritance of the Father. If only we could see with spiritual eyes what happens when we put on Christ. If only we could see the royal garments and the signet ring that He puts on us. Jesus said, "Everywhere you go, you have My authority, the name of Jesus, the family name." Everywhere you go, doors will open because of that name, the family name. It was given to you.

Our Father has commissioned a legion of powerful angels to surround us wherever we go. The Bible says that angels beyond number, myriads upon myriads, ten thousands upon ten thousands, surround us. These angels were created to be our servants.

Your Heavenly Father has given them charge over you, *"lest you dash your foot against a stone"* (Ps. 91:12 NKJV). They are with us when we put on our Father's robe and the family ring. *"No weapon formed against you shall prosper"* because you are His child, a child of God (Isa. 54:17 NKJV). Who would ever want to go back to a life without the inheritance of the children of God? You can only desire the cheap stuff of the natural world if you haven't tasted the real stuff of God's Kingdom. You would only settle for the shabby clothes that the world offers if you have never put on the Father's garment, the mantle of His anointing, the holy presence that comes on you and protects you from this world. If you could see yourself in this mantle, you would act differently. If your eyes were opened and you could see the Father's sons and daughters next to you, you would treat them differently.

As you go through life, you learn not to mess with other people's children. People will put up with a lot of stuff, but they won't let anyone mess with their children. Most gentlemen who get into a fight will play by the rules, but when the fight involves their children, there are no rules. They take out a bat, a tire wrench, whatever is available, and deal with the situation. If someone is messing with your children, there are no rules. In the same way, you are the Father's child. He will do anything to protect you if you will walk with Him and accept His love. As a matter of fact, He has done everything. The Father loved you so much that He said, "I will give My only Son. My people will ridicule Him, mock Him, spit on Him, denounce Him, and crucify Him, but I love them so much that I am going to send Him to take their place." Your Father's love, your Father's heritage, is very rich.

How many kings worry about what they are going to eat or what they are going to wear? Those details are incidental. Prince Charles is not worried about what car he is going to drive. He doesn't have a money problem. He doesn't worry about clothes. Your Father says, "Take no thought for the clothes and for the house and for the car." Take no thought. Look at the grass of the field and the birds of the air. If your Father has clothed them all, how much more will your Father clothe you? (see Matt. 6:25-27).

Christians have often thought that God wants us to do without, that we'll just be paupers and wear rags and live in shacks until we get to heaven and move into our mansions. No! We've taken it all wrong. A king doesn't have to worry about his clothes, because he has plenty. Our problem is that we've been focusing on the things that God can give us instead of focusing on Him, instead of loving Him and receiving His love.

Your Heavenly Father is pouring out His love upon you. Take it in. That love will heal your body. That love will deliver you from fear. When you taste the love of God, it delivers you from worldly rules. It takes the rules of the Pharisees and the Sadducees right out of you. Some people have been trying to please God by following a code of ethics, by following certain rules, but it doesn't work that way. All you have to do is love God and let Him love you. The Father loves you, and you can't do anything about it. He loves you, and there's nothing you can do to stop it. He's going to continue loving you.

You can try to run away from God, like Jonah did, but He won't let you go. Jonah found himself in the belly of a fish, and still God cried out to him, "I love you, Jonah, I love you. Come back. Walk with Me. Come and fellowship with Me." Your Heavenly Father loves you, and you can't do anything about it. You might as well just yield to His love. You might as well just let Him love you. Take a full blast of His love. Take it all in. Let Him drive the rules out. Let Him drive the world out. Become intoxicated and consumed by the love of God.

People have all sorts of theories about how their lives will go. It's interesting to watch single people when they start to formulate their rules and their standards. They'll say, "I'm never going to do this. I'm never going to do that. I'm going to get married when I'm 31, and we're going to have our first child when I'm

35." They go through a whole list of rules. But when the right person shows up, whoa! They can have all the rules they want, but when the right one shows up, they say, "Hang these rules. These rules are history." The same thing is true when you step into the presence of God, when you accept the inheritance that your Father has for you. You pass from a code of ethics into the reality of God's love. Love is a relationship, not a rule. And God's love is pouring out today. He's pouring out His love all across the earth. Your Heavenly Father is calling, "Come home, come home. Open your heart, and come home. Let Me love you. Let Me care for you. Let Me shelter you and provide for you. Let Me deliver you. Let Me fill you with My joy, the joy of My love, the joy of being accepted." In your Father's love is the joy of knowing that He cares for you and has an inheritance for you. He's our Heavenly Father.

CHAPTER 2

The Father's Dream

The one thing I want to get down deep into your heart is that the Father loves you. He wants to do some awesome things in your life. He loves *you* personally. He's concerned about the hurts you have and the problems you face. He knows about them, and He wants to bless you. There is an avenue that brings the blessing of God upon your life. Do you know what that avenue is? It's your heart. Father God works through your heart. He wants your heart. He looks for those who will give Him their hearts. In Proverbs 23:26, He says, *"My son [my daughter], give me your heart..."* (NKJV). When you open your heart to God and say, "Lord, I need You, I love You, I appreciate You, You're my Father," do you know what happens? His plan begins, like a seed, to be birthed inside of you. His blessing begins to germinate inside of you. As you seek after Him, that seed will grow into a mighty plant. It will live inside of you, and God will begin to live His life and His dream inside of you.

Jacob lived in the land where his father had stayed, the land of Canaan. This is the account of Jacob. Joseph, a young man of seventeen, was tending the flocks with his brothers, the sons of Bilhah and the sons of Zilpah, his father's wives, and he brought their father a bad report about them. Now Israel loved Joseph more than any of his other sons, because he had been born to him in his old age; and he made a richly ornamented robe for him. When his brothers saw that their father loved him more than any of them, they hated him and could not speak a kind word to him. Joseph had a dream, and when he told it to his brothers, they hated him all the more. He said to them, "Listen to this dream I had: We were binding sheaves of grain out in the field when suddenly my sheaf rose and stood upright, while your sheaves gathered around mine and bowed down to it." His brothers said to him, "Do you intend to reign over us? Will you actually rule us?" And they hated him all the more because of his dream and what he had said. Then he had another dream, and he told it to his brothers. "Listen," he said, "I had another dream, and this time the sun and moon and eleven stars were bowing down to me." When he told his father as well as his brothers, his father rebuked him and said, "What is this dream you had? Will your mother and I and your brothers actually come and bow down to the ground before you?" His brothers were jealous of him, but his father kept the matter in mind (Genesis 37:1-11 NIV).

In this story of Joseph's dreams, Jacob is a picture or a type of the Heavenly Father. He represents your Heavenly Father who loves you. Joseph is a picture of Jesus and a picture of us. He is the chosen son. In verse three, it says that Jacob loved his son Joseph more than his other sons. Now here is the good news: you and I are heirs of the Father God through faith in Christ Jesus, and you have become that chosen son. The Father has chosen you. You are His favorite child. You are that Joseph. Your Heavenly Father has hand-picked you, and He loves and cares for you. You are a person chosen by God!

The amazing thing is that we sometimes think that God loves and cares for certain people more than He does us. Our Father is not like a man in this sense. A man can favor one person or another, but the Father has chosen His seed, the children of Abraham through faith in Christ Jesus, and He loves each of us like a favorite child. We are heirs of God, and like Joseph was to Jacob, you are God's favorite son or daughter.

God loves you. He cares for you. Jacob had all sorts of blessings that he could bestow upon his sons. Just as Abraham loved his son Isaac and gave him everything he had, Jacob laid his hands upon Joseph and blessed him, saying, "Son, I am an old man. I am going to die. But everything that I have, that I've earned all of my life, I'm getting ready to give to you because you are my son, the son of my old age." And then Jacob gave Joseph his inheritance (see Gen 37:3-5). Father God loves you. He has chosen you to be the son or daughter of His old age so that He may lavish you with all of His blessings.

Everything that you need is in the Father's storehouse. He has healing for your body, provision for your financial needs, wholeness and peace for your family. He has a blessing in store for you. Where is it? It is in the Father's house. Your blessing can be found in His presence. You are not going to get it by pursuing the things that you need on your own. You are not going to get the Father's blessing by living life the way that the world lives. The blessings, the dreams in your heart, are waiting for you. The things that are deep down on the inside of you, that you have given up on, are still possible. Like a seed buried in the ground, God's dream for your life is still alive even though it's hidden. You may think, "I can never have a life like that." Yes, you can. It can be even better than you've imagined. The Father loves you, and He has an awesome plan for your life. Open up to His blessing. Open your heart wide and say, "Father, I want You more than anything else." You don't have to have a miserable existence. You don't have to be a spectator, looking in from the outside. God wants to give you everything He has.

Jesus came into the world so that we might receive a special gift from the Father. The gift that the Father gives us is a coat of many colors. In the story of Joseph and his brothers, that coat of many colors was a real coat. It was an expensive coat, and it got Joseph into a lot of trouble. But he had enough sense not to hang it in the closet. He had enough sense to put it on. Everywhere he went, the coat was a sign that he was the chosen one, that he was the heir. Joseph was carrying the blessing that had been passed down from Abraham to Isaac, then from Isaac to Jacob, and finally from Jacob to him.

Make a decision to wear the Father's coat. That coat is a picture of what the Father clothes us in—His anointing. It is the anointing of many colors. It is the anointing of many facets. He has a special coat prepared for you. You receive it when you get hungry for Him. Many people want to dictate how they get the coat. Some want to get the coat when they go to Bible school. Some want to get the coat when they have worked really hard for it. Others want to get the coat in a dignified way.

But this clothing is handed out when you are doing "carpet time," when you yield yourself to the presence of God. As you open your heart, He will touch you, and the glory of God will fill your heart. Many times, when you get saturated with the Holy Ghost, you may end up on the floor. Why would you end up on the floor? Because it's hard to stand up under the weight of your new coat. Your Heavenly Father starts to pour Himself out; He starts to put that coat on you.

God gave me a ministry when I first got saved and filled with the Holy Ghost. In 1979, He called me to pioneer and pastor a church in New Orleans, and I took the coat that He gave me. Since then, I have found out that God has a number of coats that He wants to put on us. He gave me a new coat in 1994. It was a coat of His presence, characterized by joy, signs, wonders, and miracles. I would have been a fool to say, "This coat is kind of loud, Lord. This color scheme is not really in style. Laughter is not popular in a lot of religious circles. Some of the people won't like it if I wear this coat every week." The temptation was to say, "I'll hang it over here. We'll have it in the back corner. For those who like this coat, we'll have special meetings."

But, no, I have decided that this is a coat that is going to stay with me all the time. It is the coat I wear when I get up in the morning. It is the coat I wear on the weekends. It is the coat I wear when I go to church, even on Sunday morning. It is the coat I wear when I play golf or spend time with my family. God the Father gave me this coat, and I am not taking it off. It is not going to the dry cleaners. I will wear it the rest of my life. I am proud of it. This coat is the mantle of the Holy Ghost. It is my Father's coat. In that mantle is everything that I need. It contains wisdom, strength, power, and revelation from God. It provides the anointing for ministry and leads people to salvation. Everything that you need is in the Father's coat, but you have to put it on.

People misunderstand the outpouring of the Holy Ghost. They look at the manifestations. As they hear laughter and crying, or see "drunkenness" or whatever happens to be taking place, people think that's all there is to it. But the outpouring is more than manifestations. It is the Father touching His people. It is His presence. The outpouring of the Holy Ghost is the Father's way of saying, "I love you." It has little to do with the manifestations and everything to do with yielding our hearts to God. We bow to Him, saying, "Oh, Father, I appreciate You so much. You are so good to me. I love You, and I open up my heart wide to you, Lord God. I want more of You."

The outpouring of the Holy Ghost does not result from our pursuit of the blessings of God. It comes from pursuing our Heavenly Father. We pursue Him and cry out, "Oh, God, I can't believe You've chosen me! I can't believe I'm Your choice! I can't believe I'm Your favorite son!" When we do this, He can't help

Himself. Just like when Jacob blessed his son Joseph, Father God says, "There is my boy; there is my girl. I want to bless him; I want to favor her. I want to shower my child with all the blessings that I have stored up." Hallelujah! He has blessed us with all spiritual blessings in the heavenly places in Christ (see Eph. 1:3).

In Christian circles today, preachers and other individuals are asking a lot of questions about churches that are experiencing the outpouring of the Holy Ghost: "Are they in the revival?" "What do they think about this revival?" "What are they doing with the revival?" I have seen three different types of responses to the outpouring from Christians. First, some are hungry, say yes, and jump in. Second, some believe the outpouring is from God, but stay on the outside observing, giving lip service to the goodness of the revival. Third, some fight it and get angry. I have heard a lot people talk about the current revival. It is one thing to talk about the outpouring of the Holy Ghost, and it is a completely different thing to experience it. It is one thing to be someone who has gone to school and learned about fishing, but it is another thing to spend your life around the marshes of southeast Louisiana and be a fisherman. The experienced fisherman knows where the fish are and how to catch them, while the fishing school graduate just has a degree. There is a big difference.

Take the coat of the anointing, and put it on. Don't wait! Start to wear it, and let it change your life. Let it affect your job. Let it affect your home. Let it affect your family. Let it affect your finances. Let it affect your ministry. Let it affect everything you have. Put on the coat. What is the coat? It is the presence of God. It is the glory of God—His mantle. The coat is the mantle that fell on Elisha when Elijah went to Heaven. It is the mantle that came on Jesus when he was baptized in the Jordan River. It is the coat that the disciples put on when the Holy Spirit was poured out in the upper room on Pentecost.

When Jesus went into the Jordan River, a mantle came upon Him. Then, when it was time for Him to go away, to return to

His Father, He promised the disciples that He would send them a new coat. In the book of John, Jesus said, in essence, "The Comforter's going to come. I'm going to go away, but I am sending another helper. The Comforter, the *Paracletos*, is going to come and be with you. Go and tarry in Jerusalem until you receive the promise of the Father."

The disciples went and waited. Then when the coat of many colors came and the Father's blessing came into that upper room, they began to speak with other tongues. They began to rejoice. They said, "Whoa, this is similar to what Jesus had, but it's different. We've got the power He had, but there is something else being featured. It has a different style."

At the beginning of this century, God began to pour out His Holy Ghost across the earth. As you look at the series of revivals that began then, you can see that each outpouring had a slightly different style. They were very similar but with slight differences. The Welsh revival, which broke out in 1903 and 1904, and was led by Evan Roberts, was very much like the revival we are currently experiencing. If you had gone to one of those Welsh meetings, you would have found tremendous joy and laughter. If you had gone to the Azuza Street revival, which broke out two years later in Los Angeles, the main manifestation you would have witnessed was speaking with other tongues.

In the 1940s, the Holy Ghost once again poured out a coat on men and women all across the earth, and that revival was characterized by healing. In videos of early 1940s services, you can see laughter and speaking in tongues, but mainly God featured the healing power of the Holy Ghost. The latter rain outpouring of the late 1940s had healing, tongues, and joy, but God was featuring prophecy. In the Charismatic renewal of the 1960s and '70s, God began to restore all sorts of things. Worship and dancing before the Lord were featured initially and then teaching, but that revival also included healing, joy, and laughter.

God features certain things when He pours out the Holy Ghost. We can't decide what those things will be. We have to go with what is happening. We have to go with Him. In 1994, the Lord looked across the earth and said, "I believe that this sorry looking bunch needs some joy." He sent His angels, and they poured out buckets of joy across the earth. He said, "I've got this coat that I like. I gave it to Evan for a while, and now I'm going to give it to My children today. Let's see if they will wear it proudly or if they will be embarrassed." I don't want to be like Joseph's brothers. I want to look like Joseph, clothed in my Father's coat. Some people may get mad when I wear my coat. They will look at it, criticize it, laugh at it, and mock it. And I will say, "This is the coat my Father gave me. I'm going to wear it proudly everywhere I go."

The dream that Joseph dreamed was not his own. His father Jacob could not grasp it. He did not like it, because like his sons, he was carnal. The dream that Joseph's Heavenly Father gave him was a dream about the future. It was a dream about his life. It was a dream that God poured out upon him as part of his anointing. Joseph's dream was part of the coat that God gave him to wear, the coat of the anointing. Joseph's brothers took off his physical coat when they sold him into slavery, and they gave it back to his dad covered with the blood of animals. But they couldn't take off the mantle that God had placed on Joseph. They could not take the coat of God's blessing. God clothed Joseph in that dream when he was 17 years old. The anointing, the dream for your life that comes from God, is in the outpouring of the Holy Ghost. That is what Joel prophesied:

> *And it will come about after this that I will pour out My Spirit on all mankind; and your sons and daughters will prophesy, your old men will dream dreams, your young men will see visions. And even on the male and female servants I will pour out My Spirit in those days* (Joel 2:28-29 NASB).

God will pour out His visions every time that you step under the anointing. When you enter His presence, His dreams will be strengthened inside of you. What are His dreams? They are the special call that He has on your life, the special plan that He has for you. God has a plan for you. You are not happenstance. He has a job for you, a special work on this earth that no one else can do, that is hand-fitted for you. Let the Father's dream live inside you! Others may try to block you from seeing the fulfillment of the dream, but you can keep it alive inside of you. You can't make it come true, but you can embrace it. Every time you see it, you can think, "This is ridiculous, but Father, I'm just going to live in this dream. This is the funniest dream I've ever seen in my life, but Lord, I believe." In the fullness of time, at the appointed moment, your dream will come true.

The Father has a blessing that He pours out. Abraham gave it to Isaac; Isaac gave it to Jacob, and Jacob gave it to his sons. In Genesis 49, Jacob prophesied over his 12 sons, proclaiming the blessing of God upon their lives. He spoke of the inheritance that God was going to give to them, to their children, and to their children's children. God has an inheritance for you. It is a rich inheritance. It is an inheritance that He has reserved for His children.

When you are born into a natural family, you receive a blessing through the possessions and privileges that belong to you as a member of that family. For example, you receive privileges and blessings if you are born into a Christian family. If your parents happen to be a man and woman of God, who love the Lord and walk in the ways of the Lord, you are privileged. I did not have that kind of blessing in my life. But the good news is that even though I was not born into a Christian family, God has passed down to me the heritage of my forefathers. The Heavenly Father has a sense of humor. Our God sits in the heavens and laughs. When my grandmother was dying, I found out that two generations ago my great grandfathers on both sides of my family were Pentecostal preachers. My family tried to hide that heritage from me. Those forefathers were outcasts from the family, unloved and unaccepted. But God gave me their heritage, and I am proud of it. It is part of the coat my Father gave me. It is the dream my Heavenly Father gave to me.

When God gave me a dream, in 1978, to start a church, my wife and I didn't have anything. We had no jobs, no money, absolutely nothing. I was in Georgia, in October 1978, when the Holy Ghost gave me this dream. I shared it with several people, and as a result, I was called on the carpet. A lot of preachers got mad at me when I told them what God had called me to do. Later, officials from our fellowship called me into their offices and criticized me. They said, "Do you think you're going to be the only church in town? We've heard that you think you're going to have a church of thousands of people. Who do you think you are?" They were offended, and they criticized me. I said, "I can't help it; the Father told me, and He gave me the dream."

Other people may not like the dreams that God gives us, but that is not our choice. We cannot be affected by human opinions, by what people think and what people do. We have to wear the coat, take our Father's dream, and be proud of it. Living with the Father's dream for your life is not always pleasing to the flesh. God birthed my dream, but it didn't happen in the time frame that I expected. I thought it would happen much quicker. But, guess what? It has happened, and it is happening. Every day I have to turn off the negative voices. I had to do it when I was 26, and I have to do it now. Turn off the voice of criticism. Turn off the voice of doubt and unbelief, the voice of Joseph's brothers who want to throw you down a well. Turn off those negative voices and say, "I'm going to wear this coat that my Father gave me. I'm going to wear it proudly. I'm going to walk with this dream alive in my heart all the days of my life."

In Genesis 49:22, as Jacob was dying, he prophesied over Joseph. Remember what Joseph had gone through to get to that point: his brothers sold him to slave traders because of his dreams, and he spent at least 13 years in an Egyptian prison. Then God gave him the interpretation to Pharaoh's dream about seven years of plenty and seven years of famine. At the end of those 14 years, Joseph's brothers came crawling to him, and he provided food for them. Joseph's dream about his brothers and his father bowing down to him came true. When his father was dying in Egypt, Joseph was one of the most powerful men on the earth, second only to Pharaoh. Jacob prophesied over his son:

> *Joseph is a fruitful bough, even a fruitful bough by a well; whose branches run over the wall: the archers have sorely grieved him, and shot at him, and hated him: but his bow abode in strength, and the arms of his hands were made strong by the hands of the mighty God of Jacob; (from thence is the Shepherd, the stone of Israel:) even by the God of thy father who shall help thee; and by the Almighty, who shall bless thee with blessings of heaven above, blessings of the deep that lieth below, blessings of the breasts and of the womb: the blessings of thy father have prevailed above the blessing of my progenitors unto the utmost bound of the everlasting hills: they shall be on the head of Joseph, and on the crown of the head of him who was separate from his brethren* (Genesis 49:22-26).

I want to live near that spring like Joseph did. I want to be like a fruitful vine near a spring, like a vine whose branches climb over a wall. The vine keeps growing even if the wall gets in the way. The branches keep growing right over the top. Just as the skilled archers could not weaken Joseph, I want to remain steady and strong in the face of all those who attack me, who would try to destroy the dream that God has put in my heart. With the help of the Shepherd, the Rock of Israel, I plan to stand up to the voices of doubt and criticism and to receive all the blessings my Heavenly Father has to give me.

God has given you His Word, just as He gave Joseph His Word. He has prophesied over you with His Word. If you open your heart and live in His presence, you will be a fruitful vine, and you will be blessed. If you open your heart to Him, no one can do anything to keep you from receiving His blessings. It will happen. Your dreams will come to pass. Remember that no matter what anyone does, Jesus is coming back. Yes, on a white horse, with fire in His eyes and a sword in His hand, He is coming back. Will you ride with Him in that last day? The Lord is coming back for the Church of His people, His chosen sons and His chosen daughters. I want to live in this life under the Father's blessing as I await the day of Jesus' coming. Archers' arrows can't touch me. The world can't stop me. I will see the fulfillment of God's dream for my life as I go forward under the anointing of His favor and blessing.

CHAPTER 3

The Father's House

How precious is Your loving-kindness, O God! Therefore the children of men put their trust under the shadow of Your wings. They are abundantly satisfied with the fullness of Your house, and You give them drink from the river of Your pleasures. For with You is the fountain of life; in Your light we see light (Psalm 36:7-9 NKJV).

When I first read this verse about "the fullness of Your house," I wanted to figure out what David was talking about. As I started investigating, I looked up the phrase "abundantly satisfied." Sometimes Bible translators get nervous about what things really mean because the original language is so strong. In this verse, "*abundantly satisfied*" means "to be saturated, satisfied, fulfilled, or intoxicated." If we read it the way David intended, this passage would say, "They are intoxicated; they are saturated; they are filled with the fullness of Your house. And You give them drink from the river of Your pleasures. For with You is the fountain of life and in Your light we see light."

What exactly is the Father's house? What do you find in the Father's house? Children often take their possessions for granted. My dad was a very successful businessman. He had pretty much everything he wanted. He drove a nice car, lived in an upper middle class neighborhood, played golf at the country club, and enjoyed all that good stuff. I was raised in that environment, and I had pretty much whatever I wanted. I thought that was the way everyone lived. I didn't really appreciate how good things were until I got married and didn't have anything. My wife and I really looked forward to special days when we went to my father's house because he had a really big house. He had lots of food. We could go in the pantry or refrigerator and get anything we wanted. He had an awesome yard in the back and a pool table upstairs. It was wonderful, but afterwards we had to go back to our little apartment where we had nothing, where we had an empty cupboard, an empty refrigerator, and a tiny backyard that was just big enough for the dog to mess up. So I used to really enjoy going to my father's house.

Now David got a radical revelation of God. To the normal Jewish mind, God was an austere God that you couldn't talk to. He was ready to slap you, ready to judge you, ready to pour fire on your head, ready to send you to hell if you didn't get your act together. But that's not what David saw. When David looked up and saw the Father, he saw mercy. He saw loving kindness. He saw the goodness of God. And he said, "*One thing have I desired of the Lord, and that will I seek; that I may dwell in the house of the Lord all the days of my life, to behold the beauty of the Lord, and to inquire in his temple*" (Ps. 27:4 NKJV). When you step into the reality of the presence of God, when you start to experience His touch upon your life, you can begin to enjoy the privileges—the awesome, endless, abundant privileges that you have received as a child of the Heavenly Father. Whether you realize it or not, you have a rich Dad. He's really rich. He has a really big house, and you don't have to wait until you die to hang around the Father's house. You can move in today.

The prodigal son lived in a big house. He had everything he needed. He had a room of his own, plenty of clothes, plenty of food. He could eat any time he wanted. He had a wonderful place to hang out. Everything he wanted was at his fingertips, but he was angry inside. He wanted his dad's inheritance right away. He didn't want to wait until his dad died, so he asked for his inheritance early and ran off and squandered it on riotous living. The prodigal son eventually found himself living with pigs, and his mind turned back to the awesome house that he was raised in. He said, "Oh, I wish I could be back in my father's house again. If I could only see my own bedroom once again and move back in. If I could only show up at that table, I'm sure they're having roast turkey for dinner tonight, with dressing and everything, and here I am eating pig food. Oh, for one more moment back in my father's house." So the prodigal son started the journey back to his father's house, not knowing what to think or what to expect. Was he to get a good whipping and be sent out to live with the servants? He thought that was what he deserved: "Oh Lord, just give me one of your servants' meals, let me sleep in the slave quarters. Lord, anything, I just don't want to live in that pig sty anymore." He made his way back, willing to take his punishment.

As he came down the road, his father saw him from a long way off. His father was waiting and picked up his robe and began to run to meet his son. He ran down the road. The son confessed, "Father, I have sinned against you and against heaven. I'm no longer worthy to be called your son." But his father said, "Put the robe on him, put the ring on his finger, put the sandals on his feet, kill the fatted calf. We're going to celebrate! Come, son, come back into your father's house. There's plenty of room for you at the father's table" (see Luke 15:11-32). Just like the prodigal son, you don't have to live in the backyard anymore. You don't have to live in the slave quarters anymore. Come into the Father's house and live. Come out of the shacks of this world. Come out of the residence of the Philistines, and live in the Father's house, in the place of His presence. The most special thing about the story of the prodigal son is that the house that he returned to was where the father lived. The father was home.

Today the Father is waiting for you to step into His presence. He's saying, "Come on, child, come into My presence. Come to Me. I want to show you all that I have planned for you. Take My yoke upon you for it's easy, and My burden is light. Come move into My house. I have a special place at the table for you. You can eat until you're satisfied. I have a special bedroom for you, a special set of clothes for you, and a special dream that I want to put to your heart." The Father is calling us now. He doesn't want us to remain outside. People have gotten hung up on John 14:2, which says, *"In My Father's house are many mansions; if it were not so would have told you. I go to prepare a place for you"* (NKJV). Everyone's waiting on the outside for their mansion in heaven. But the Father's house is here, now! Where is it? It's in His presence. Move into His presence. Step into the presence of God. Quit hanging around on the outside. Come on into the Father's house.

When God raised Jesus from the dead, He gave Him an inheritance. In Philippians 2:9-11, Paul writes that, as part of that inheritance, He *"was given a name that is above every name, that at the name of Jesus every knee should bow...and that every tongue should confess..."* (NKJV). You have an inheritance available, too. What will happen when you move into the Father's house? You will inherit all that your Heavenly Father has prepared for you: His name, His clothing, and His promise of provision and abundance. Inheritance is an awesome thing. After my dad died, he left an inheritance for all of his children. My brother and sister were able to move into houses with the money they received. That's pretty nice. I was able to buy cars and other things. That's wonderful. That's an inheritance. How foolish to never show up to get it just because you didn't think it was yours. Our Heavenly Father has an awesome inheritance set aside for us, and we don't have to wait until we die to get it. It became ours when Jesus died on the cross. It became the last will and testament of our Lord Jesus Christ.

When you move into the Father's house, you take on the Father's name. *"That at the name of Jesus every knee shall bow and every tongue confess..."* Oh, I know a place. It's a place of refuge. It's a place where the name of Jesus is. It's a place of protection. It's my strong tower. It protects me from sickness and disease and tragedy. It protects me from poverty and from the snare of the fowler. Isaiah 54:17 says that no weapon formed against me shall prosper. Why? Because I'm living in my Father's house, and no devil can get into the Father's house. I've got His name written upon my head. I'm not afraid any more. Whose name are you carrying? Whose name are you walking around in? Think about it. Your Father is inside of you. The glory of God is inside of you. Demons live in the spiritual realm, so when God comes on the scene, they know it. The only problem is, do you know it? When you're walking around in the Father's house, with the Father's anointing, with the Father's name, no demon can stay in front of you. They have to flee. If you have a lot of problems, then move into the Father's house. Your problems won't go away just because you prayed the sinner's prayer. You have to move into the Father's house.

I'm walking around with my Father's name. When you are part of the family, all kinds of privileges come your way. So many of God's children are not taking their place, not enjoying their privileges, not walking in the authority of Jesus' name, not living in their Father's house. They're running around in their own strength, in their own power, and in their own name. The saddest thing is that some people don't live in the Father's house, but they want to confess all of the Father's promises, such as, "*My God shall supply all your needs according to his riches in glory by Christ Jesus*" (Phil. 4:19 NKJV). Receiving God's blessings is about more than just quoting Scripture. Where do you live? What's your address? Move to 777 New Jerusalem Avenue! God has given us His name as our inheritance, and more!

As part of my inheritance, my dad left me some funky-looking clothing, which I never could use, some strange-looking leisure suits, and one-piece overalls. I could never have worn those clothes, but my dad gave them to me anyway. Contrary to my earthly dad's clothing, our heavenly Father's clothing is always in style.

When I moved into the Father's house, He gave me an inheritance that included clothes: I put on the garment of praise, the robe of righteousness, and the mantle of the anointing of His Spirit. When you move into the Father's house, you just slip on His garments. They are tailor-made for you. You can wear these clothes all the days of your life. In Isaiah 61:3, the Lord said to put on "*the garment of praise for the spirit of heaviness....*" A life clothed in praise is much better than the alternative: complaining, grumbling, negativity, anger, and discouragement. Take off those clothes, and put on your new ones. When you put on the new clothes, you will go around singing the new song of the Holy Ghost, singing in tongues, singing the song of joy. So when you put on the Father's clothes, you are saying, "I am abundantly satisfied, intoxicated with His love, filled with the new wine of the Holy Ghost.

I have this new coat, and it's called the garment of praise. Everywhere I go, I can't stop praising His name. I can't shut my mouth. I can't stop glorifying Him." If you're wearing that garment when Sunday night comes, you're going to find your feet dancing to church instead of dancing to wherever else people go on Sunday. On Wednesday night you'll have the coat on again. You'll be wearing it all the time.

I've moved into my Father's house. This is the way that I want to live my life now. Don't just visit Him on Sunday morning for an hour. Move on in! Come on into the Father's house! When you leave the church service, don't check the garment of praise with the ushers before you go out the door. Put it on! Wear it in your car! Take it into your house!

Instead of listening to that sad old song the world is singing, put on the song of the Lord in your house. Put on the garment of praise, and start wearing it around your house. Put on that Holy Ghost music in your house and in your car. Start dancing around wearing that garment of praise. Take off the spirit of heaviness. It's a much better way to live. Sleep in your clothes tonight!

The Father has given you a robe to wear, the robe of righteousness that has been washed in the blood of Jesus. It means no more guilt and no more shame. When the prodigal son came home after running with the whores, after wasting all his daddy's money, his dad said, "Put these new clothes on him; put that robe of righteousness on him." We walk around and the angels say, "Look at that. He's wearing the Father's robe of righteousness. He looks just like Jesus." Don't take that robe off. You can't check your coat at the door, or you'll find yourself doing things you shouldn't be doing. I don't want to take my robe off. I'm going to wear it to bed. I'm wearing the robe of righteousness. I'm washed in the blood of Jesus, and I have a brand new nature that is clean, white, spotless, and holy.

I put on Dad's clothes when I go to His house. I'm wearing the Father's shoes, His pants, His coat, His robe, His hat. I'm clothed with the garment of praise and with the robe of righteousness. But God has another coat that He wants me to put on too. It's the coat that He gave to His son Joseph. It's the coat of many colors. It's the coat of the anointing of the Holy Ghost; so I'm also wearing the coat of His mantle, or His anointing. When telling His disciples about the coming anointing, Jesus said, "*Most assuredly, I say to you, he who believes in Me, the works that I do he will do also; and greater works than these he will do, because I go to My Father*" (John 14:12 NKJV). Later He told them, "*Behold, I send the Promise of My Father upon you; but tarry in the city of Jerusalem until you are endued with power from on high*" (Luke 24:49 NKJV). This promised power was the anointing that the disciples received on the day of Pentecost.

When the anointing comes, we should put it on and say, "I'm going to wear these clothes all the days of my life. I'll never take them off. I'll never take off my garment of praise. I'll never take off my robe of righteousness. I'll never take off this mantle of the anointing. I'm going to walk in it all the days of my life. I think I'm just going to hangout with David in the Father's house." David knew the pleasures of the house of God. He wrote, "*For a day in thy courts is better than a thousand. I had rather be a doorkeeper in the house of my God, than to dwell in the tents of wickedness*" (Ps. 84:10). Remembering that the Father's house is the place of His tangible presence, we constantly need to check our hearts. When we can't sit still in church or spend time in the presence of God, what else are we going to do? Go back to the tents of wickedness? Never! Instead, start hanging out in the Father's house.

My dad used to get upset when we'd visit him and leave too quickly. He'd always call and ask us to bring the kids and come visit for a while. As I got busy in ministry, that was harder and harder to do. Now that he has passed away, I often wish that I could go visit him, but I can't. Today I have another house that I can go to, that I can live in. It's an awesome house. It's my heavenly Father's house, the place of His presence.

Another privilege of the Father's house is that He spreads the table for you. He serves the greatest Thanksgiving dinner ever. You sit there and eat that awesome meal, tasting of His Word, feeding on the manna from Heaven. You feed your soul with the bread of His presence. Until you see that the Word is full of His presence, you will have little understanding of it. The Bible is not an instruction manual that we recite from our heads. It's what we feed on. In Matthew 4:4, Jesus said, *"Man shall not live by bread alone, but by every word that proceeds from the mouth of God"* (NKJV). We feed on the Word, and it becomes alive inside of us. John wrote, *"In the beginning was the Word....And the Word became flesh and dwelt among us, and we beheld His glory...full of grace and truth"* (John 1:1,14 NKJV). Jesus is the Word of God.

When you begin to feast on the Word of God, Jesus comes inside of you. You feast on Him. When you open the Word, you will begin to see Jesus walking on the pages. The Bible will come alive. Walking through the pages of Matthew, Mark, Luke, and John, you will see Jesus healing the sick, casting out devils, feeding the poor, and raising the dead. You will see Him in the Acts of the Apostles, as the Holy Ghost falls on Peter, James, John, and Paul. You will see Jesus in the epistles, writing His Word to us, encouraging and building up His Church, the Body of Christ. You will see Him in the book of Revelation: His eyes like lightning, His words like a mighty, flaming sword that comes out of His mouth, His face shining like the sun at noonday strength. See Jesus in the Word of God. Feed on His presence by dwelling in the Father's house.

In our Heavenly Father's house, He also has a giant wine cellar. When you enter this wine cellar, you can't even see the end of it. If you walk around, you'll see a giant vat where the wine is bottled; and if you fall in, you'll get lost. It has no bottom. This bottomless wine vat is filled with the new wine of God's presence. Come with me to my Father's house. Belly up to the Father's bar; He has some new wine on tap today. He wants you to drink in His presence and to be filled with the Holy Ghost anointing so that you won't care about the problems of the world. Then you won't care about who's running for president or about what the mayor said or about the prognostications for the future. Just say, "I'm going to live in my Father's house. I'm going to drink my Father's wine. I'm going to have a nice big drink of the Holy Ghost."

As you live like this, things will begin to go right for you. The whole world can be falling apart, but everything will be wonderful for you, and you won't be able to figure out why. Everyone else in your type of business will be going bankrupt, but you'll be blessed. What's the secret? Come with me to the Father's house, and I'll show you His awesome wine cellar. Our Father has provided us with a heritage of provision and abundance!

I still have a long way to go, but I'm starting to realize that I have missed too much of life. Life in the Father's house is a blast! People have the wrong idea about our Father. They think being a Christian means that you miss out on so much. I'm missing out on bars, hookers, AIDS, divorce—boy, I really am missing a lot! Instead, I've decided to move into my Father's house, where He holds a continuous, huge Holy Ghost party.

When people ask me when I'm going to start acting serious again, I tell them, "Never!" This party is going on for eternity. It's never going to stop. What can we do today? Let's plan this day and pack it with fun; pack it with joy; pack it with life. Let's have one big party with God. His house has a table full of food and a huge Holy Ghost wine vat that you can swim in. The giant river of His presence runs through the living room. It's the river of glory. It's so clean, so refreshing. Drink from this clear, living water, and you'll feel something strange in your belly. When you feel it bubble up inside of you, you may think it's just carbonation, but it is actually living water. Come to the Father's house, and receive all of His inheritance. Our Father's house is a place of blessing, a place of His presence.

CHAPTER 4

The Father's Blessing

Joseph is a fruitful bough, even a fruitful bough by a well; whose branches run over the wall: the archers have sorely grieved him, and shot at him, and hated him: but his bow abode in strength, and the arms of his hands were made strong by the hands of the mighty God of Jacob; (from thence is the shepherd, the stone of Israel:) even by the God of thy father, who shall help thee; and by the Almighty, who shall bless thee with blessings of heaven above, blessings of the deep that lieth under, blessings of the breasts, and of the womb: the blessings of thy father have prevailed above the blessings of my progenitors unto the utmost bound of the everlasting hills: they shall be on the head of Joseph, and on the crown of the head of him that was separate from his brethren (Genesis 49:22-26).

On a recent trip to Boston, I kept reading over this passage of Scripture, which speaks of Jacob's love for his son Joseph. Joseph's life illustrates that the anointing of God upon your life, doesn't guarantee that you won't have any problems. Problems may come your way. In fact, problems definitely will come your way. But, as Jacob prophesied, the branches of Joseph's life grew until they stretched over the wall. They could not be stopped by the forces of the world. Even though Joseph's own brothers hated him and persecuted him, he was able to fulfill God's plan for his life.

Following God doesn't mean that you're going to win a popularity contest. Persecution comes because of the anointing. Joseph's brothers hated him because of the coat that his father gave him. Even though he was in prison for many years as a result of the evil that they did to him, Joseph's hands stayed strong, and he enjoyed the blessings of God.

Genesis 49:25 talks about three kinds of blessings: the *"blessings of heaven above,"* the *"blessings of the deep that lieth under,"* and the *"blessings of the breasts and of the womb."* When Jacob spoke these blessings over Joseph, he was also speaking them over each one of us. As we consider the blessings that were upon the favorite son of Jacob, we must remember that Jacob was the grandson of Abraham, and Joseph was Abraham's great-grandson. God gave a promise to Abraham that he was going to be blessed, and that promise was passed down from generation to generation. In the New Testament, Paul writes that we become the sons of Abraham not through our physical birth, but through our spiritual birth. Today you are as much a son of the promise as Joseph was. We are children of the promise. The blessings of Abraham are for us!

Genesis 37:3 tells us that Jacob loved Joseph more than all of his children. I believe that God put this passage in the Bible for each of us. He wants you to know that He loves you more than He loves anybody else. I don't know how this is possible, but somehow God loves each one of us as His favorite child. When you get the revelation that you are the "Joseph" of God, that you are the chosen seed and the favorite son, your life will begin to change. You'll begin walking in the favor of the Almighty God. Jacob prophesied over Joseph, but this prophecy is also a word for you from the Lord. You are Joseph. This promise is just as real as if Jesus was sitting here today, putting His hand upon you, and saying, "Thus sayeth the Lord of Hosts, My son, My daughter...." He's prophesying to you today, and He's saying that He has blessings from Heaven for you, that you can reach out and take them as yours. It's that coat, that mantle. The promised blessing is precious, new, and fresh every day. It's a special anointing that is coming down from God in Heaven just for you!

Joseph put on his coat. In the natural sense, it was probably the ugliest coat around. It may not have been in style, but it was God's coat. It was the blessing from Heaven. Joseph wore that coat everywhere he went. It changed his life, and it changed his countenance. It changed the way that he thought about himself. Joseph did not walk in his own abilities or trust in his own strength. The anointing that comes from above levels your pride and keeps you from trusting in yourself. Instead, you trust in the anointing that's coming down upon you. You draw upon the mantle of God's presence and blessings every day of your life. You come to depend upon the mantle, the anointing, the presence of God, the blessings from heaven above.

Those blessings change your life. They change the way your business goes. They change the way your ministry goes. They change the way your family goes. When you begin to live your life like Joseph did, you continually walk in blessing and anointing. The wonderful thing is that this special blessing is for you. It's not just for the TV preachers. It's not just for the preachers who fill stadiums. It's not just for the big-name evangelists. This anointing is for you! You are Joseph!

I used to minister strictly by the Word, and I didn't understand the anointing. I knew it existed, but I thought it was reserved for the chosen few, for the Oral Roberts and the Benny Hinns of this world. I thought I was just a left-out preacher who had to walk by faith. I didn't know that God had made an anointing available for me. When I first began to experience the anointing falling upon me, I took it. And as I experienced life under that anointing, I began to see that I was God's favorite son, that I was His Joseph, and that He had a coat for me. The wonderful thing is that this anointing is not just for the preacher. This anointing is for the welder, for the pipe fitter, and for the dress maker. It's for the maintenance man, the business owner, the student, and the musician. It's the blessing from Heaven above.

The Lord showed me something else about the first part of this prophecy, about the blessings from above. God raises up families in the Body of Christ—local churches and groups of local churches. There were twelve tribes in the nation of Israel, and I believe they were very different from each other. I'm beginning to realize that, in the same way, God has established clear tribes in the Body of Christ. They don't act the same, worship the same, or preach the same. They're culturally different. I'm not talking about biological tribes. I'm talking about a different spiritual family, a different anointing that comes upon people. Psalm 133 talks about an anointing of unity that comes from above. It came down upon Aaron's head and dripped down on his garments. The blessing from above comes upon us individually, but it also comes to us as we surrender ourselves to the Body of Christ that God has called us to serve in. He places us in families.

Over the past few years, God has given me the opportunity to travel and to worship in many different places. Even though differences exist everywhere I go, I'm able to enjoy the worship and the people. However I realize that they are not my family. It's like when you go to visit friends: you enjoy being with them for a while, but you're still at someone else's house. They're not your family. The churches that I visit have wonderful worship and a powerful anointing, but they're not my family. God is not only raising up a local church at Victory Fellowship, but He's raising up a fellowship of ministers and ministries that are linked together.

They're not necessarily linked together because of their own desires, but because God has willed it. God is raising up a spiritual family. His blessing is coming upon our church and our ministry, and it's spreading down upon the ministers and ministries that are associating with us. It's wonderful. It's a family anointing.

Specific blessings are associated with particular churches. For example, God has chosen to emphasize certain things at Victory Fellowship. My wife and I used to be "church growth specialists." We were the experts who try to make their churches grow by figuring out what people like. The idea is that if you sing the songs that people like, preach the messages that people like, have the programs that people like, and provide for everyone's different needs (from jazzercise to cappuccino), a big crowd will come to your church. Yes, a big crowd may come, but God will be offended. Several years ago, my wife and I determined not to make decisions according to what we thought would make our church grow, but according to the anointing that God has placed upon our ministry. We determined to follow the cloud of God's glory. Because of that decision, the Lord has placed His hand upon Victory Fellowship and upon everyone who identifies with our church. Because of their family rights, the people that God gathers into our church family begin to carry upon their own lives the same mantle that we have.

Asher was different than Joseph; Joseph was different than Reuben, and Reuben was different than Judah. Their children were different. Their families were different. And God made it to be that way. We can't compare our families with other families. You're born into one, and that's it. Just go with it and say, "Lord, thank you for this family. It may be a weird-looking family, but I'm happy with it." That's your blessing from above.

In Genesis 49, when Jacob spoke of the blessings of the deep, the meaning of the word he used relates to "deep waters." A water table lies under the surface of the earth, and springs flow deep within the earth. God also created underground rivers.

These water sources beneath the surface represent a blessing that comes to us from God. The mantle of God's anointing comes upon us, but once we enter the flow of God, things change. Suddenly the anointing comes not only upon us, but also from deep down inside of us (see John 7:38). In John 4:13-14, we read about a spring, a fountain at Jacob's well, where a Samaritan woman came to draw water. Abraham originally dug the well, and Isaac re-dug it after the Philistines filled it with dirt. Jacob dug it out a third time. The Samaritan woman came to drink from Jacob's well, but when she met Jesus she left her water pot behind. She no longer needed to draw from a natural well because she had found a new source of water deep down beneath the surface.

When you enter God's anointing and the river of His presence, you will find an unending spring inside of you. When you surrender to the Holy Spirit, a fountain will spring up that can satisfy you whenever you want a drink. If you wake up in the middle of the night and hold your belly and begin to speak in tongues, a fountain will bubble up, and you'll feel it gurgling deep down on the inside. A burst of joy will shoot up inside of you. You have to be willing to pray in tongues and willing to release the joy.

As you begin to get into the flow of God's anointing, blessings will start to be released. Blessings from the deep places in your life will surge up inside of you, and suddenly you'll have Holy Ghost ideas. Creative things will happen. Joy, peace, love, freedom, and deliverance will spring up from within you. These are the blessings from the deep.

God's Kingdom is spiritual. You don't grab it with your hands or figure it out with your mind. It isn't the result of applied principles that lead to a successful life. God's blessings from the deep flow from a person who wants to live inside of you, who wants to radiate those blessings out of your innermost being. Religious people don't want you to tap into this deep source. They are offended when you do. Religious people prefer decent worship that's orderly and controlled. It offends the religious program when the Holy Ghost stirs up inside of you. Man can't control what flows out of the well within you, and that's exactly how God wants it. Suddenly the anointing of God is inside of you, springing up from the deep. You become a river in the desert. You become the rock that traveled around in the wilderness, following the Israelites. Everywhere that rock went a river came out of it. As you learn to live under the anointing and to tap into the well within you, you will become a living stone that carries the river of God's presence. That hidden river is promised to every one of the children of Abraham. It flows out of those who are yielded to God. That river holds the blessings from the deep.

It may seem strange that Jacob would prophesy the "blessings of the breasts and of the womb" over a man. But Jacob prophesied an awesome spiritual blessing, as well as the blessing of physical reproduction and children. Every son of Joseph is given the ability to reproduce spiritual children. Every one of us has that ability, not just the evangelists and the preachers. We carry inside of us blessings from above and blessings from the deep so that we can pour these blessings into others.

Inside Abraham's loins were generations and nations. They were inside him by faith. Inside every child of God are spiritual seeds. Those seeds are the souls of the people that you can touch as you walk through life under the anointing of God. They are the seeds of people who need to be born again. The Christian life is much more than attending church and paying your tithe. Souls are inside of you, waiting to be birthed. Birthing souls is not difficult. In fact, it becomes very easy and natural. You'll find souls falling into your lap, if you'll yield to the anointing of the Holy Ghost. Just yield to His presence and make yourself available when the simple opportunities come along. The Lord has planted souls all around you, souls that are destined to come to Him through you.

I remember one of the first people that I knew who came to the Lord right after I got saved. I didn't know much about the Bible, except maybe John 3:16. I was a brand new Christian on fire for God, and I worked at K-Mart, loading and unloading trucks. I'd bring my Bible to work and read it on my ten-minute lunch break. People would sit with me, but they scattered as soon as the Bible came out. Before I knew it, I was eating by myself, feeling rejected and persecuted. Sometimes my boss would push a heavy cart at me to see if I would curse when it hit me. I hated working there.

Finally I found a "real" job, shoveling manure at a chicken ranch. One Saturday on my day off, I went into a Bible bookstore and saw one of my former co-workers from K-Mart. He came up to me and said, "I just wanted to thank you." He told me that he had watched me at work to see how I would respond to the people on the job who rejected and persecuted me. He ended up getting saved and going to Bible school because of my witness!

All I did at K-Mart was read my Bible and say, "I'm a Christian." I didn't know the four spiritual laws. I didn't even know that the four spiritual laws existed. I didn't know how to witness. I hadn't taken any classes on leading people to Jesus. All I did was refuse to compromise and listen to their stupid, dirty stories. I was just a Christian, following the Spirit of God, and from this a young man was birthed into spiritual life. There are souls inside of you that are waiting to be born too.

It's easy to have children in the natural world and it's the same spiritually. You just have to be willing to yield to God. Just stand up as a Christian and be willing to say, "Don't talk like that around me. That offends me." Just say, "I'm a Christian." By reading your Bible and going to church, you are being a witness. Even though the people around you may not respond properly at the time, you can be sure that God is moving in their lives!

As you go through life, it is essential that you learn to enjoy the blessings of God—the blessings from above, from the deep, and from the womb. Revival is inside of you. The revival that has already begun around the world and the revival that is coming next are already inside of you. There are souls, waiting for salvation, inside of you. What keeps all of these blessings from coming forth? Fear. You will miss these blessings if you don't take advantage of the tangible anointing that is available at church, in prayer lines, and anywhere else that God's Spirit is being poured out. You have to carry the anointing with you when you go home, take it in your car and to your job. As you become the fruitful vine that climbs over the walls, searching for the life to come, the blessings of the breasts will nurture your spiritual children.

Before the current revival, many of us believed that we had to do certain things to please God. We can all get that way as Christians. It's easy to think that if you get into the ministry, go to church a certain number of times, and pay your tithe, you can work your way into Heaven. However, that's not what the Kingdom of Heaven is about. It's about getting into the presence of God and loving Him. It's about letting God touch you and change you. As you receive the blessings that He has for you, you will naturally share them with someone that you're sitting next to or working with. God has blessings from Heaven, blessings from the deep, and blessings of the womb and breasts. These blessings rest upon the spiritual sons and daughters of Abraham, and they are waiting for you. Don't feel pressured. Just yield to the mighty stream of God. Receive the anointing that He wants to pour upon you; seek the river that He has placed inside of you. As you do, God will release from within your womb the mighty multitude of your unborn spiritual children. Open yourself today to all the blessings that your Heavenly Father has promised you!

CHAPTER 5

The Father's Love

In the story of the prodigal son, there are two brothers. One of them left home, messed up, and repented. The other one never did anything wrong, but he criticized his brother who had done wrong and repented. Each of us is like one of these brothers. The good news is that your heavenly Father loves you when you serve Him and when you mess up. His love is unconditional. It doesn't increase when you act better. He loves you no matter what. We get stuck believing in a conditional love that says, "I love you if you do a good job and perform well, and I'm angry at you if you don't." But our Father just loves us.

Luke 15:1 says that the tax collectors and sinners all gathered around to hear Jesus. In the Jewish culture of Jesus' time, tax collectors were considered to be the lowest rung on the ladder of society. When the tax collectors and sinners gathered around to hear Jesus, the Pharisees and the teachers of the law muttered, *"This man receives sinners and eats with them"* (Luke 15:2 NKJV). Times haven't changed. Both heathens and religious people walked the earth in Jesus' time, just as they do today. Both groups were listening to Him, but the religious people got upset because Jesus associated with the sinners. To help explain the situation, He told them the parable of the lost son.

This story is not just about a man and his two sons. It is actually about the heavenly Father and two types of people: the sinners who know that they are sinners and the "religious" people who think that they are better than the sinners.

To further illustrate the point, He told them this story, "A man had two sons. When the younger told his father, 'I want my share of your estate now instead of waiting until you die!' his father agreed to divide his wealth between his sons. A few days later this younger son packed all his belongings and took a trip to a distant land and there he wasted all his money on wild living. About the time his money ran out, a great famine swept over the land and he began to starve. And he persuaded a local farmer to hire him to feed his pigs. The boy became so hungry that even the pods he was feeding the pigs looked good to him. But no one gave him anything. And when he finally came to his senses he said to himself, 'At home even the hired men have food to spare and here I am dying for hunger. I will go home to my father and say, "Father, I have sinned against both heaven and you and I am no longer worthy to be called your son. Please take me on as a hired man."' So he returned home to his father and while he was still a long distance away, his father saw him coming, and filled with love and compassion he ran to his son, embraced him and kissed him. And his son said to him, 'Father I have sinned against both heaven and you and I'm no longer worthy of being called your son.' But his father said to the servants, 'Quick, bring the finest robe in the house and put it on him. Get a ring for his finger and sandals for his feet and kill the calf which we've been fattening in the pen. We must celebrate with a feast for this son of mine was dead and is now returned to life. He was lost but now he's found.' So the party began. Meanwhile the older son was in the fields working; when he returned home he asked one of the servants what was going on. 'Your brother is back,' he was told, 'and your father's killed the calf we were fattening and has prepared a great feast. We were celebrating because of his safe return.' And the older brother was angry and wouldn't go in, but his father came out and begged him. But he replied, 'All these years I have worked hard for you and never once refused to do a single thing you told me to do; and in all that time you never gave me even one young goat for a feast with my friends. Yet when this son of yours comes back after squandering your money on prostitutes, you celebrate by killing the finest calf we have.' His father said to him, 'Look, dear son, you and I are very close and everything I have is yours, but we had to celebrate this happy day. For your brother was dead and is come back to life, and he was lost but now he's found'" (Luke 15:11-32 NLT).

This story captures what the Bible is all about. Until you come to the conclusion that you are the son who ran away and squandered his Father's inheritance, you will never be able to rejoice and be glad. Everything that you have has been given to you by your Father. Everything! This whole earth is filled with the Father's goods. It is His, and we are His children. The younger son said to his father, "Give me my share of the estate," so the father divided his property between his two sons. He gave his younger son all of his inheritance. This is similar to what happens to many of our famous musicians and singers who get their start playing and singing for the Lord. They take their inheritance, their musical gift, and they go out and start doing their own thing, playing and singing for themselves, living for themselves, living for what they can get out of the gift that God has given them. That is what happened to the younger son.

He went to a distant country and wasted everything that he had on wild living. After he had spent everything, a famine came into the land, and he began to be in need. He went to the field to feed the pigs, and he longed to fill his stomach with the pods. He was in need and became hungry. Finally, he began to recognize the need in his life. Until you come to the place where you recognize that you are needy, that you need God, you will always be hungry. Until you realize that you will never be self-sufficient, that you can't just float through life, that you can't just be a good person and go to church occasionally, you will never enter the fullness of His love.

Why did Jesus use the example of the prodigal son? He was saying that the people of this world are trying to satisfy their spiritual hunger by eating pig food. The lost son looked at the pig food and came to his senses. Some of you are eating pig food. I'm telling you the truth. It is your regular diet. You get up in the morning, and the first thing you do is turn on the television—pig food. You start consuming it. Oink, Oink, Oink. You think it's so tasty. You go to work and tell all the funny jokes. Oink, Oink, Oink. You gather at the coffee pot and listen to the stories about the weekend conquests. Oink, Oink, Oink. You laugh at them, like an old pig, wallowing in the mud with all the other pigs.

The problem is that your eyes are blinded, and you cannot see that you are in with the pigs. Then you go to church, because you are a good church-going pig, and when you get there, some of the people are actually eating the Father's food. You get mad at them because they are excited about the Father's food. You just want to sit like a bump on a log, enduring the service, so that you can go home and eat some more pig food. "He longed to fill his stomach." Oh, you want some of that pig food. You can't wait to get some more of it.

The younger son longed to fill his stomach with the pods that the pigs were eating. Then he came to his senses. He looked around and asked himself what he was doing surrounded by pigs. He said,

> *How many of my father's hired men have food to spare and here I am starving to death? I will set out and go back to my father and say to him, "Father I have sinned against heaven and against you, I am no longer worthy to be called your son, make me like one of your hired men." So he got up and went to his father* (Luke 15:17-20 NIV).

This is what must take place in your life. You have to say, "I was wrong." That is the hardest thing for people to do. People want to say, "Oh, it is actually my father's fault because we were a dysfunctional family. It wasn't my fault." No, it is your fault. It's not your father's fault; it's not your mother's fault; it's not somebody else's fault. To the white people, it's not the black people's fault. And to the black people, it's not the white people's fault. It's not the government's fault. It's not the aliens' fault. Take responsibility for the mess that you're in. You are the reason that you're in a pig sty.

The good news is that you can get out of it. Now, I know that in the natural world we are born into different situations. Some of us are born with more privileges and more opportunities than others. But when you get filled with the Holy Ghost, when you get Jesus in your life, everything changes. You have to come to your senses and say, "I'm not going to eat pig food any more. I'm not going to live like other people live. I'm not going to blame other people. Like the prodigal son, I'm going to go and say, 'I was wrong, Father. It was my fault. Father, I have sinned against Heaven and against You. I am no longer worthy to be called Your son. Make me like one of Your servants.'"

The younger son humbled himself. He bowed down. He removed the arrogance, pride, haughtiness, and hardness that he had lived in. He humbled himself and said, "I was wrong. Forgive me." The problem is that we look around and see everyone else's faults and everyone else's sins. And there are plenty of them to see. But if you do that, you will never change yourself. You will just continue walking around with all the other pigs. Don't worry about whether or not other people are wrong. Your problem is you. Get your eyes off of the other pigs. Say, "I was wrong. I am wrong. Father, forgive me. Change me, Lord."

When the prodigal son made the long journey back home, I'm sure he thought about turning around. He didn't want to go back and say he was wrong, but he was hungry. He hadn't eaten in a long time, and when you are hungry, you will do things you normally wouldn't do. Are you hungry enough yet? Or do you need to go out and wallow with the pigs some more? The younger son was on his way home, and while he was still a long way off, his father saw him. His father, looking down the road, saw his son's familiar walk.

His father was filled with compassion for him. Remember, the father in this story represents our heavenly Father. He is good. He's filled with mercy and tenderness. He loves us. He loves us enough to let us go out and do what we want. He even lets us enjoy His bounty while we are out there doing what we want. While the prodigal son was still a long way off, his father saw him and was filled with compassion for him. He ran to his son. The father didn't give his son a long lecture but threw his arms around him. He kissed him. The son just asked if he could become a servant. He said, "I don't really deserve anything. I just want to eat."

However, the father said to his servants, "Quick, bring the best robe and put it on him; put a ring on his finger and sandals on his feet." He ordered that the fattened calf be brought and killed, "for this son of mine was dead and is alive. He was lost and is found." Everyone began to celebrate. What an awesome display of mercy and love!

This is what the Father does when we humble ourselves. When we say, "Father, I was wrong. Lord, forgive me for wasting Your blessings," He puts His arms around us. He begins to kiss us. He loves us. Then He takes out His best robe and puts it on us. My Father gave me my coat. I didn't deserve it. I went to Him smelling like a pig, with pig food all over me, and He gave me His best robe. The coat that my Father gave me is like the one Joseph's father gave him. What is that coat? That coat is His anointing. It's the Father's presence. He covers us with His presence. That coat is the coat of righteousness, a garment of praise for the spirit of heaviness. It's His coat of glory. We don't deserve it. But when we go to Him and say, "I was wrong," He gives us His coat. He puts it on us.

Some people go to church to see the preacher wearing the garment. They want to wallow with the pigs all week long and then go to church and worship the coat on Sunday. Instead of worshipping the coat, put it on. Your Father is giving it to you. Take His coat, and wear it proudly everywhere you go. It's His glory. It's His presence. People won't like it when you wear the coat around, because they won't smell the same way that you smell. When the coat comes into the room, suddenly their party will start to stink, and they'll know it. Everything will smell good until you show up. When you arrive, they'll be shocked into reality, and they'll see that they are wallowing in pig mess. They'll say, "Get that coat out of here! We don't like it."

The father said, "Everything that I have belongs to him, even though he wasted his inheritance. This is my son, and everything that I have belongs to him. He's part of the family." Our Heavenly Father says the same thing to us. He says, "I'm a God who is full of mercy. You're a son of God. You're My son." He gives us His robe and His ring, and He puts shoes on our feet. Our Father also gives us a job.

Our job is to wear our new shoes everywhere, telling people how wonderful our Father is, how He loves us, and how He cares for us. Our job is to tell about how He clothed us with His robe of glory, how He put His covenant ring on us, and how He gave us all His promises even though we didn't deserve them. We should run everywhere, telling everyone that our Father is a good God, that His mercy endures forever.

When you have a real experience with the Lord, when you get touched by God and you start serving Him, you might be tempted to forget where you used to live. It is easy to forget the pigpen. As you start working in the fields, you begin to criticize other people for the way they dress, talk, and live. You become filled with pride and lose the touch of God. All you have is a bunch of religion.

Our works are not going to get us into the Kingdom. In case you haven't noticed, we are not in the Kingdom Hall of the Jehovah's Witnesses. Those poor folks are trying to work their way into heaven, and it can't be done. There is only one way to get into heaven: you need to fall on your face, crying out, "Father, I have sinned. Please forgive me." Then your Father will pick you up and hug you and put His robe on you.

After the servants brought the fattened calf, they threw a big party. Everyone was eating and dancing and singing and rejoicing. The prodigal son's father was so happy that nothing else mattered. His son had returned! Meanwhile, the older son was working in the field. As he came near the father's house, he heard the sound of music and dancing. The older son went to the house, called one of the servants, and asked him what was going on. "Your brother has come home," he was told. This servant doesn't sound to me like a very loyal servant. It sounds like he was full of rebellion: "Your brother has come back. Remember that sorry guy? Can you believe it? Your father killed the fattened calf. I can't believe your father killed the fattened calf! He never did anything like that for you."

When he heard about the reason for the celebration, the older brother became angry and refused to go to the party. "I'm not going in there with all that music and dancing. Those people are nuts." His father went out and pleaded with him to join the party, but he replied, "Look, all these years I have been slaving away for you, and I've never disobeyed your orders. Yet you never gave me anything. You never even gave me a young goat so that I could celebrate with my friends." What an attitude! He didn't even want to celebrate with his father. Then the older son accused his father: "I can't believe you gave him that money. This son of yours squandered your property. You're an idiot. He squandered your money with prostitutes. Then he came home, and you killed the fattened calf for him." The father didn't even get angry at his Pharisee son.

I have been both of these sons. From time to time, I am still both of these sons. The father loved both of his sons:

> *"My son," the father said, "you are always with me and everything I have is yours, but we have to cele-brate and be glad because this brother of yours was dead, and now he is alive again. He was lost, and is found"* (Luke 15:31-32 NIV).

The Bible's message is clear: God loves you. He's a Father, and He loves you. The Bible is not a book of rules and regulations about what you can and can't do. It is a book about love. The Bible is a book about a Father and His children. John 3:16 says, *"God so loved the world that He gave His only begotten Son, that whoever believes in Him will not perish, but have everlasting life"* (NKJV). Every day the Father is touching people's hearts. He can touch your heart, too.

People have tried to describe the outpouring of the Holy Ghost that is sweeping the world today. Our church has been experiencing it since 1994. People have tried to label it, but it doesn't matter what label you use. The whole point of it is this: our Father is saying, "I love you." He is pouring His love into our hearts. This outpouring is all about opening our hearts and accepting the Father's love. It's about being filled with His passion and falling in love with Him.

When you are touched by the real presence of God, the fire of your love for Him will burn in your heart. You won't be lukewarm.

You will say, "I don't know about anything else. I don't understand why people shake or why people laugh. All I know is that once I was lost, and now I am found." I don't know many things, but I do know that I love Jesus and that He loves me. A fire burns in my heart that can't be extinguished. God wants to put a fire like that in you today.

This is an incredible time to be alive. I used to wish that I had been alive during Jesus' lifetime on earth or during one of the times of great spiritual awakening. However, now I realize that we live in the greatest time of all. This is the final chapter, the time of the end. The Lord is preparing the world for His return with an awesome outpouring of His love.

Are you ready? Have you been captured by His love? Can you feel His presence surrounding you? The Father is desperate. He is desperately and hopelessly lovesick. He has fallen head-over-heels in love with you. What is He longing for? He is waiting for you to respond. Open your heart today. Let God's love pour into you.

As you reach out to God, stepping into the realms of the Holy Spirit, you will receive the greatest gift of all. What is this gift? It is the Father's promise for you, from before the foundation of the world. It is the promise of His love. Open your heart to your heavenly Father, and let Him shower His blessings upon you. Receive your full inheritance as a child of God. Let His dream for your life become a reality. Make a decision to dwell in the house of the Lord every day of your life!

Ministry Contacts

To contact the author, Frank Bailey, please use
the following addresses:

Correspondence address:

Full Gospel Christian Church
5708 Airline Drive
Metairie, LA 70003

E-mail Address:

fbailey@victoryfellowship.net
hmoore@victoryfellowship.net

Telephone:

504-733-5005

Ministry Website:

Full Gospel Christian Church, d/b/a Victory Fellowship
www.victoryfellowship.net

Additional copies of this book and other
book titles from DESTINY IMAGE are
available at your local bookstore.

Call toll-free: 1-800-722-6774.

Send a request for a catalog to:

Destiny Image₍ᵣ₎ Publishers, Inc.

P.O. Box 310
Shippensburg, PA 17257-0310

*"Speaking to the Purposes of God for This
Generation and for the Generations to Come"*

For a complete list of our titles,
visit us at www.destinyimage.com